SCUBA DIVING SAFETY

Dan Orr ◼ Eric Douglas

SCUBA DIVING SAFETY

Dan Orr ◼ Eric Douglas

HUMAN KINETICS

Library of Congress Cataloging-in-Publication Data

Orr, Dan, 1947-
  Scuba diving safety / Dan Orr, Eric Douglas.
      p. cm.
  Includes bibliographical references and index.
  ISBN-13: 978-0-7360-5251-1 (soft cover)
  ISBN-10: 0-7360-5251-8 (soft cover)
  1. Scuba diving--Safety measures. I. Douglas, Eric, 1967- II. Title.
  GV838.674.S24O77 2007
  797.23--dc22   2007003374

ISBN-10: 0-7360-5251-8
ISBN-13: 978-0-7360-5251-1

This publication is written and published to provide accurate and authoritative information relevant to the subject matter presented. It is published and sold with the understanding that the author and publisher are not engaged in rendering legal, medical, or other professional services by reason of their authorship or publication of this work. If medical or other expert assistance is required, the services of a competent professional person should be sought. The opinions in this book are those of the authors and do not necessarily reflect the opinions or policies of any organizations with which the authors are affiliated. This book employs masculine and feminine pronouns in descriptions of various scenarios; this practice is not intended to imply that either gender is more likely to be involved in specific situations.

Notice: Permission to reproduce the following material is granted to instructors and agencies who have purchased *Scuba Diving Safety*: pp. 38 to 40. The reproduction of other parts of this book is expressly forbidden by the above copyright notice. Persons or agencies who have not purchased *Scuba Diving Safety* may not reproduce any material.

Acquisitions Editor: Jana Hunter; **Developmental Editor:** Heather Healy; **Assistant Editors:** Laura Koritz and Carla Zych; **Copyeditor:** Patsy Fortney; **Proofreader:** Bethany J. Bentley; **Indexer:** Nan N. Badgett; **Permission Manager:** Carly Breeding; **Graphic Designer:** Robert Reuther; **Graphic Artist:** Kim McFarland; **Photo Office Assistant:** Jason Allen; **Cover Designer:** Keith Blomberg; **Photographer (cover):** Steve Simonsen; **Photographers (interior):** Dan Orr, Eric Douglas, and Betty Orr, unless otherwise noted; **Art Manager:** Kelly Hendren; **Illustrator:** Rick Melvin; **Printer:** Versa Press

We thank Bluestone Dive Resort in Thomasville, North Carolina, and Water World in Durham, North Carolina, for assistance in providing the locations for the photo shoots for this book.

Human Kinetics books are available at special discounts for bulk purchase. Special editions or book excerpts can also be created to specification. For details, contact the Special Sales Manager at Human Kinetics.

Printed in the United States of America   10   9   8   7   6   5   4   3   2   1

Human Kinetics
Web site: www.HumanKinetics.com

United States: Human Kinetics
P.O. Box 5076
Champaign, IL 61825-5076
800-747-4457
e-mail: humank@hkusa.com

Canada: Human Kinetics
475 Devonshire Road Unit 100
Windsor, ON N8Y 2L5
800-465-7301 (in Canada only)
e-mail: orders@hkcanada.com

Europe: Human Kinetics
107 Bradford Road
Stanningley
Leeds LS28 6AT, United Kingdom
+44 (0) 113 255 5665
e-mail: hk@hkeurope.com

Australia: Human Kinetics
57A Price Avenue
Lower Mitcham, South Australia 5062
08 8372 0999
e-mail: liaw@hkaustralia.com

New Zealand: Human Kinetics
Division of Sports Distributors NZ Ltd.
P.O. Box 300 226 Albany
North Shore City
Auckland
0064 9 448 1207
e-mail: info@humankinetics.co.nz

I dedicate this book to my wife and life partner, Betty, who always provides creative inspiration and support when it is needed most; to Julia, Ron, Ryan, and Lindsay so they may learn from my experiences and safely enjoy all the wonders diving has to offer; and to my mentor, Dr. Lee H. Somers, as partial fulfillment of a promise to share my thoughts and ideas with others.

—Dan Orr

This book is dedicated to Ralph Douglas for encouraging me to be curious and learn about everything that interested me. Thanks, Dad. And thanks for becoming a dive buddy. That made all the difference.

—Eric Douglas

CONTENTS

PREFACE

I had the pleasure of being in the audience at the International Conference on Underwater Education (IQ) in Santa Ana, California, when Al Pierce received the prestigious Leonard Greenstone Award for Contributions to Diving Safety from the National Association of Underwater Instructors (NAUI) in 1987. In his acceptance speech, Pierce said that many in the diving community had influenced his career and that any success he had was really due to the efforts of others who had come before him. His words were "I accept this award for all those who have contributed to my success. I am here today, having reached the pinnacle of my career, having stood on the shoulders of giants. Those giants are all those who contributed to the field of scuba rescue."

Scuba rescue, like all other disciplines, is the result of an accumulation of knowledge and skills, developed over time and passed on through courses and training programs as individual contributions become incorporated into diver training as standard procedures.

Rescue techniques, like most other emergency skills taught in recreational diving courses, are complex psychomotor skills. As such, they require some level of initial overlearning, or redundancy, as well as periodic reinforcement so that a rescuer can apply them quickly and effectively without having to think through each step. Divers should practice rudimentary rescue skills such as self-rescue and buddy assistance repeatedly during entry-level scuba training. Once certified, divers should practice these skills at every opportunity. I strongly recommend that divers enhance and expand their rescue skills through continuing education. Each recreational scuba training association offers training specifically focusing on diver rescue and accident management. Typical courses include Diver Rescue, Scuba Lifesaving and Accident Management (SLAM), and Stress and Rescue. Whatever name they go by, these courses and training programs are highly recommended for any diver who wants to be able to provide assistance to a buddy or other diver in distress.

It is my hope that those who read this book will appreciate the value of being prepared to manage a diving or diving-related emergency. Of course, there is some level of risk in everything we do. As safety-conscious divers, we do our best to mitigate risk through complete and comprehensive *planning,* detailed and coordinated *preparation,* and constant *practice* to reinforce all critical safety skills. By following the safety guidelines provided in this book and by your certifying organization, you can significantly reduce the risk of accident or injury and, at the same time, increase the pleasure derived from every diving experience.

Rescue skills, like all skills and techniques in diving, must be adaptable to a variety of circumstances. When you learn self-rescue techniques or practice coming to the aid of a buddy during entry-level scuba training, those skills are generally performed in a calm, comfortable swimming pool with virtually unlimited visibility. Because you may be called on to perform these skills in actual open-water diving conditions, in limited visibility or in cold water with currents and wave action, it is essential that your diving and rescue skills become almost second nature. The kind of ability required to perform effectively under adverse conditions comes only from practice and reinforcement of both basic diving and rescue skills.

Accident management must be more than just a reaction; it must involve a finely tuned and coordinated set of actions that have been practiced and reinforced to the point that, in the unlikely event of an accident, you act almost instinctively to provide assistance to a diving partner. Everything you and your diving partner do to prepare for every dive should increase the likelihood that, if something were to occur, you would recognize what's happening, successfully manage the situation, and treat it as one more step in your evolution as a safe and competent diver. After all, the best rescue is the one you never have to make!

This book, as Al Pierce would say, is the result of work done by many giants in recreational diving, and specifically in the fields of rescue and accident management. Because of their experiences in applying theory to the best and worst possible conditions, we now enjoy new and better techniques. I encourage everyone who reads this book to share his or her rescue and accident management experiences with others. It is through this process that rescue skills are improved, perfected, and passed on to future generations of giants.

—Dan Orr

INTRODUCTION

Rarely can a dive accident or injury be tied directly to a single event. From the Divers Alert Network's annual *Report on Decompression Illness, Diving Fatalities and Project Dive Exploration,* we know that a dive injury can occur without any error on the part of the diver. Accidents certainly can happen when someone makes a catastrophic mistake, but more often, they begin with a small problem that leads to other problems. The problems then compound until a diver becomes caught up in a cascade of stress and panic, and gets into real trouble.

According to the most recent Divers Alert Network (DAN) accident data, diving equipment was a factor in only 6 percent of dive fatalities (Divers Alert Network, 2006). Modern equipment rarely fails, but when a chain of events starts, the diver might worry that the equipment has failed or is going to fail. For example, consider a diver who is working very hard at depth, swimming against a strong current. This exertion causes him to hyperventilate. The hyperventilation, possibly exacerbated by the increased breathing gas density at depth, increases his breathing workload, causing him to believe that his regulator is not performing properly. This may cause the diver to abruptly abort the dive and escape to the surface, letting fear drive him to a rapid ascent that could in turn result in an air embolism, decompression sickness (DCS), or drowning.

Causes of Diving Accidents

Divers Alert Network has studied and collected reports on dive injuries and fatalities since 1987 in an attempt to identify the causes of diving injuries and fatalities in order to make diving safer. This information is published annually as part of the organization's *Report of Decompression Illness, Diving Fatalities and Project Dive Exploration.* Each year DAN receives reports of approximately 1,000 cases of decompression illness and 80 to 100 fatalities involving U.S. and Canadian residents diving around the world. DAN reviews and verifies the information from these cases before they are published in the annual report.

Dive injuries are the result of many circumstances and events, including environmental, medical, and procedural factors. Environmental factors include any natural conditions such as cold water, currents or wave action, depth, and visibility. Medical factors include obesity, smoking, alcohol use, cardiovascular disease or high blood pressure, breathing difficulty (both temporary and chronic), dehydration, and a general lack of physical fitness. Procedural factors include buoyancy control, air supply issues such as being out of air or low on air, rapid ascents, missed decompression, a lack of recent familiarity with basic or critical emergency skills, and improper use of dive equipment. Recent DAN accident data (2006) show that dive conditions such as deep and cold water diving, even when the divers are prepared for it, can significantly increase the risk of decompression illness.

The DAN data show that the largest percentage of divers who are injured each year have only an open-water diver certification. This is understandable given that this is the largest certification group. According to DAN's data, divers with more experience seem to be less likely to be injured, and the likelihood of injury is reduced even further among those with recent experience. This is probably due to the fact that these divers have had more recent practice and have a greater familiarity with basic and critical emergency skills. Divers with more experience are exposed to the same stressors as divers with less experience; perhaps the crucial difference is that the more experienced divers are able to recognize the problem, solve it, and complete the dive. Proper training and recent familiarity with critical and essential diving skills reduces the likelihood that a problem during the dive will initiate a cascade of events that could spell disaster. The DAN data support the idea that inexperience or lack of recent practice plays a role in dive accidents. In the most recent DAN accident data, 40 percent of the men and 50 percent of the women had made fewer than 20 dives in the last 12 months.

Following is a list of problems identified by injured divers involved in dive accidents as reported in the 2005 edition of the *Report of Decompression Illness, Diving Fatalities and Project Dive Exploration*. Although the numbers may vary slightly from year to year, the same problems are reported nearly every year.

1. Rapid ascent (This is the most common problem; it was identified in nearly 20 percent of dive accidents.)
2. The next three most common problems were as follows:
   - Heavy exertion (about 12 percent). This can be caused by doing more work than planned or physically prepared for during a dive. Currents and wave action are the primary culprits.
   - Feeling cold (10 percent). This can be caused by inadequate exposure protection during a dive or continuing a dive beyond the point of physical comfort.
   - Missed decompression (10 percent). This involves missing required decompression stops by overstaying the planned bottom time.
3. A small number of accidents were caused by the following:
   - Nausea or dizziness (8 percent)
   - Problems with equipment (7 percent)
   - Out of air (5 percent)
   - Shortness of breath (3 percent)
   - Physical injury or trauma (1 percent)

The figures for problems related to dive fatalities look a bit different. Equipment problems were believed to have contributed to the fatality in 20 of 89 instances studied by DAN in 2005. Of those, problems with buoyancy compensation devices (BCDs) and regulators were the most common. In most of the accident situations, it was difficult, if not impossible, to determine the exact cause of the equipment-related problem. The actual cause may not have been a mechanical problem, but rather a procedural one in which the diver may not have completed an equipment check prior to entering the water or may have lacked recent experience with the specific design.

Dr. George Harpur of Tobermory, Ontario, Canada, said, "We are not able to document a single case in which equipment failure directly caused a diver's death or injury. It has been the diver's response to the problem which results in the pathology" (personal communication in 2002). The available data on diving accidents leads to the same conclusion: It is generally diver error rather than any design flaw that causes a diving accident.

Diving and Stress

Many factors, both physical and psychological, can cause divers to feel stressed underwater. Diving is an exciting sport and inherently involves a bit of stress. The act of diving can make the diver more aware of his surroundings. Seeing a shark or another large fish, or descending on a shipwreck for the first time, can excite divers and increase their pulse rate. This physical stress is a part of the adventure of the dive—the controlled thrill that many are seeking from the diving experience.

© National Geographic/Getty Images

Controlled thrills, such as seeing a stingray, contribute to the excitement of a dive.

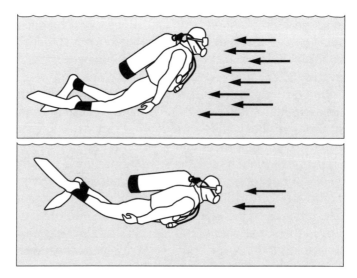

FIGURE 1   Improper equipment can increase the workload of a diver by making it harder to maintain proper position.

Other stressors on a dive might be considered procedural. For example, in moving from saltwater to freshwater, divers who use the same exposure protection and weights may be overweighted and therefore struggle throughout the dive, constantly kicking to keep themselves off the bottom (see figure 1). Or divers may overinflate their BCD to compensate for the weight, thereby increasing their workload and breathing rate. On a deep dive, the increased gas density may force divers to work harder to breathe. This procedure-related struggling and labored breathing make the divers feel uncomfortable and stressed.

Similarly, by presenting a larger surface area to the water as they swim forward, divers increase their workload and their stress level. An awkward swimming position significantly increases the workload. According to research conducted by Dr. Glen Egstrom from UCLA (e-mail on June 14, 2006), each increase in surface area increases the workload required to maintain a constant speed by its square. So, doubling the frontal surface area in swimming increases the workload fourfold. Tripling the surface area while moving through the water requires nine times more energy to maintain a constant speed.

In order to reduce drag, workload, and physical stress, divers should be as streamlined as possible. They should minimize the air in their BCD and configure all equipment so that their hoses are tight against the body. In addition, divers should always make adjustments in weight and exposure protection when moving from one type of environment to another.

Divers must also contend with psychological stressors. Fear of the unknown, fear of an animal, discomfort with a dive situation, or even fear of surfacing (arising from a lack of confidence in the dive plan or level of preparedness) can create stress. During one dive–boat excursion, a diver saw a rather small shark for the first time and her breathing increased so much that she was down to 500 PSI in no time and had to return to the boat. The divemaster and crew referred to that sighting as the 2,000-pound (as in PSI) shark.

Another significant stressor in diving is task loading. When divers attempt to do too much on a dive, or deal with too many issues or tasks, they may become overwhelmed and make an incorrect decision. Task loading can also occur when divers have too many firsts on a dive: the first time using a new piece of equipment; the first time leading a dive; or the first time diving at night, at depth, or in a current. One of these special situations or firsts would normally be no problem; two or more together could increase stress as well as risk.

Diving and Panic

Panic is the body's means of rescuing us from a problem. It gives us the strength to fight or flee, depending on which response is more appropriate. Panic also leads to some physical manifestations such as perceptual narrowing, irrational and uncoordinated movements, or a shutdown in which we remain still in spite of increasing danger or needed action, basically frozen with fear. Panic can also play a part in a rescue. Divers need to be prepared to deal with a possible panicking diver every time they attempt a rescue.

Panic is different from apprehension, although one may lead to another. Apprehension is that subconscious voice that warns against doing something or going somewhere. Panic is what happens when a situation creates feelings that go beyond apprehension. Panic is unreasoning fear causing undirected, uncontrolled, or unproductive activity. According to the *Diagnostic and Statistical Manual of Mental Disorders,* 4th edition (DSM IV; American Psychiatric Association, 1994), a panic attack is a discrete period of intense fear or discomfort, in which four (or more) of the following symptoms developed abruptly and reached a peak within 10 minutes:

1. Palpitations, pounding heart, or accelerated heart rate
2. Sweating
3. Trembling or shaking
4. Sensation of shortness of breath or smothering
5. Feeling of choking
6. Chest pain or discomfort
7. Nausea or abdominal distress
8. Feeling dizzy, unsteady, lightheaded, or faint
9. Derealization (feelings of unreality) or depersonalization (being detached from oneself)
10. Fear of losing control or going crazy
11. Fear of dying
12. Paresthesias
13. Chills or hot flashes

When panic sets in, people lose control of their performance and possibly of the situation. The severe physiological changes that accompany panic during a dive may, in turn, contribute to further loss of control—such as when hyperventilation leads to ineffectual swimming and a loss of buoyancy. This syndrome can be seen in divers who claw at the surface and use ineffectual leg movements.

A diver in full panic probably won't recognize that a rescuer is attempting to help and can cause the rescuer harm. There are several warning signs to indicate that a diver may be about to panic. Rescuers need to be aware of these signs, which include the following:

- A wide-eyed look
- Rapid breathing
- Swimming movements becoming jerky and irregular
- Attempts to claw to the surface
- Holding head above the water (high-treading)
- Removing mask and spitting out the regulator or rejecting other equipment

Something that often accompanies panic and panic situations is perceptual narrowing. As stress and panic increase, the five senses collapse around a single point, usually vision. Even powerful stimuli from other senses are simply filtered out. Even more significantly, the visual field may narrow by as much as 70 percent—creating tunnel vision. So, not only is the injured diver limited to one sense, but that one sense is greatly reduced. Under these conditions, a rescuer will have to be extremely careful when dealing with this diver.

Along with perceptual narrowing, divers may also suffer from response narrowing, whereby their ability to react to the situation is compromised. Under extreme stress, divers tend to respond with the behaviors that have been overlearned and frequently practiced.

Ultimately, training is the best means of reducing the likelihood of panic. In a 2003 study, David Colvard, MD, and Lynn Colvard, PhD, documented the experiences of panic in more than 12,000 certified divers. They found that 81 percent of the men and 75 percent of the women who experienced a panic episode remembered their training and used that training to overcome the situation. Of the men and women who had a panic episode underwater, 15 percent made a rapid or an uncontrolled ascent to the surface. Fortunately, only 5 percent of the men and 4 percent of the women reported signs and symptoms of decompression illness, and only 1 percent of the men and 2 percent of the women needed recompression treatment. Another testament to the power of training is that 82 percent of the men and 80 percent of the women decided they needed more training after their panic incident. They realized they needed to improve their skills before resuming diving.

Clearly, safe diving is attainable through frequent, specific practice and training.

PART I

Safety Planning

1

Safety and Prevention

Is recreational scuba diving safe? Given that the term *safe*, by definition, means "free of risk or harm," is anything really safe? Clearly, everything we do has an element of risk. Scuba diving is no different. Therefore, all safety-conscious divers must be able to identify the risks and develop ways to reduce or eliminate them.

The frequency of scuba-diving-related injuries and fatalities is difficult to determine. Divers Alert Network (DAN), a nonprofit diving safety organization, has collected information on dive accidents and fatalities since 1987. However, DAN receives this information from facilities that treat the most serious diving-related injuries, namely, decompression sickness or arterial gas embolism (also known collectively as decompression illness or DCI). No data is available concerning other non-life-threatening injuries such as barotrauma to the ears or sinuses or bites, stings, and other diving-related trauma.

Determining the actual incidence of injury for scuba diving has been, and continues to be, somewhat problematic. No reliable data exist that quantify the number of certified recreational divers or the number of dives made annually by divers in the United States, Canada, or around the world. Although estimates can vary greatly, the Sporting Goods Manufacturers Association indicated that 2.9 million people participated in scuba diving in 2005.

Data collected by DAN involving U.S. and Canadian citizens diving worldwide indicate that approximately 1,000 cases of DCI and fewer than 100 fatalities (see figures 1.1 and 1.2) are reported each year (Divers Alert Network, 2006). Without knowing the actual number of incidents and the number of dives, however, we cannot accurately determine the frequency of injury for recreational scuba diving.

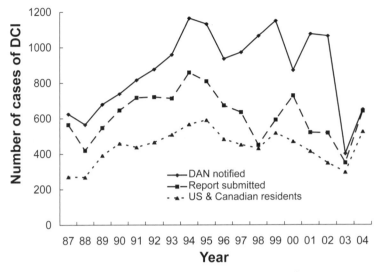

FIGURE 1.1   Yearly comparison of number of cases of DCI.
Reprinted with permission of Divers Alert Network.

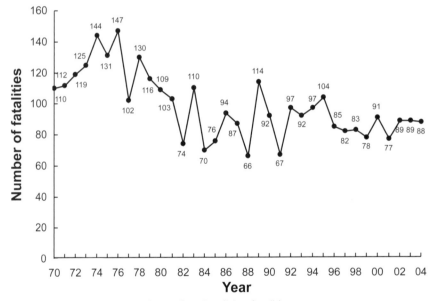

FIGURE 1.2   Yearly comparison of scuba diving fatalities.
Reprinted with permission of Divers Alert Network.

Recently, the recreational diving community in the province of British Columbia, Canada, made an attempt to determine the incidence of injuries and fatalities. They embarked on an ambitious project, called the Abacus Project (Ladd, Stepan, and Stevens, 2002), to quantify, with the greatest degree of accuracy possible, the number of dives made during a defined period. The project involved a cooperative effort by the majority of dive operations providing cylinder fills during an 18-month period. The data from each facility were later analyzed and compared to the number of reported cases of DCI and diving-related fatalities occurring within the province. The results showed the incidence of DCI at 9.57 and the incidence of death at 2.05 for every 100,000 dives. Ultimately, the combined risk for death or DCI was 11.62 incidents per 100,000 dives. The results of this project reinforced the accuracy of the estimated incidence of injury and fatality that had been suggested by DAN for many years.

The DAN data, supported by the data from the Abacus Project, show that although diving accidents and fatalities do occur, they are relatively rare. Statistically speaking, a case can certainly be made that recreational scuba diving is probably as safe or safer than some other leisure activities. Therefore, most divers can expect to enjoy their entire diving careers without ever being involved in, or having firsthand experience with, a diving accident or injury. That does not mean, however, that divers should not continue to do everything possible to identify and reduce potential risks while scuba diving—or be fully prepared to manage an emergency situation if it were to occur to themselves, a diving companion, or another diver.

Dive Site Knowledge

Knowledge is one of the most important keys to managing risks. The more you know about the dive or dives you are about to make, the better prepared you can be. In reality, this is no different from preparing for a vacation or any other leisure trip. Knowing everything you can about where you are going can help you prepare for any challenges that may arise that could reduce your fun. After all, one reason you chose the sport in the first place may have been to enjoy the silence, beauty, and grandeur of the underwater world. This next dive could be the experience of a lifetime; why risk spoiling it by failing to prepare?

To prepare to dive a new location, find out when the diving conditions are best (time of day or year), the water temperature, the marine life that may be present, possible hazards such as shifting currents or rapidly changing tides, and the best way and location to enter the water. You should also get basic information such as compass headings to the actual site, as well as depths and bottom conditions (sand, rock, or mud bottom). Unexpected changes in any of these factors may influence your enjoyment of the dive and potentially increase your risk. You should also check to see whether any special require-ments or regulations exist before leaving home. If you wish to dive without the requisite level of experience, some dive operators may require that you dive under the direct supervision of an instructor or experienced dive guide. This is one of several good reasons to keep an up-to-date dive log with detailed records of your diving experiences and training.

If you've never been there, how do you find out about prospective new dive sites? A host of resources are available to help divers learn about new places to dive. In the privacy and comfort of your own home or office, you can surf the Internet and find just about anything you want to know about virtually any dive destination in the world. You can also make contact and communicate directly with other divers who have been there through scuba forums and chat rooms. Libraries and bookstores also offer a variety of destination guides and photography books that can give you some unique insights into possible dive locations. Other outstanding sources of information are local dive resorts, charter boat operators, dive retailers, and dive clubs. Not only can these sources provide you with valuable information, but they can also help make some of the arrangements for you and introduce you to prospective dive partners if you are traveling alone.

© Bruce Coleman

Dive-site research can lead you to great experiences in amazing locations.

Certification and Experience Requirements

Looking back at the natural progression of your training and certification, you may remember that you were a bit anxious when you first went from poolside to breathing on scuba underwater. Then, with the help of a patient and knowledgeable instructor, you gradually gained experience and confidence. Having reached the end of the certification process, you were qualified as an open-water diver, but you were only prepared and qualified to dive in a specific type of open water.

This really defines the difference between certification and qualification in diving. Certification is the process by which you move toward completing the requirements for receiving recognition as a diver at a particular skill level, whether it is open water, advanced open water, or some specialty area. Qualification, on the other hand, has to do directly with your diving experiences. In other words, certification refers to your scuba education, while qualification refers to the manner and extent to which you put that education into practice in real world settings. Recent experience is especially relevant; you are only as qualified as the timing and success of your last dive indicate.

Unless you live near the coast, your initial open-water experiences were probably in a quarry or lake. Therefore, at the end of that certification process, you were a certified diver with experience in cold, calm freshwater, with some limited visibility. You also probably had some experience wearing a wetsuit and limited experience with buoyancy control in freshwater. The confidence you gained and the experiences you had were all centered on one particular type of diving environment.

If you decide that your next dive will be in the warm waters of the Florida Keys, you must be prepared to modify your skills to cope with an entirely different diving environment. You would do that to make sure that your experience will be a safe and an enjoyable one and, hopefully, reinforce your desire to continue with scuba diving as a lifelong leisure activity. The first trip to a new diving environment or dive site can be truly wondrous. The reverse can also be true, however. Failing to prepare for the changes in going from freshwater to saltwater or vice versa could turn an otherwise fascinating experience into a disaster.

One thing stands out in the DAN accident statistics in terms of diver experience. Those with limited open-water experience, with no recent familiarity with the critical skills required for the dive, are most at risk (see figure 1.3). Many of the problems cited stem from a lack of recent experience, which in turn leads to buoyancy control problems, running out of air, and a lack of familiarity with the necessary dive equipment. A common mistake inexperienced divers make is using the same weights and exposure protection when they go from freshwater to saltwater or vice versa. As mentioned previously, it is always a good idea to get help when doing something new. Specialty training courses, supervised trips offered by instructors or dive retailers, and

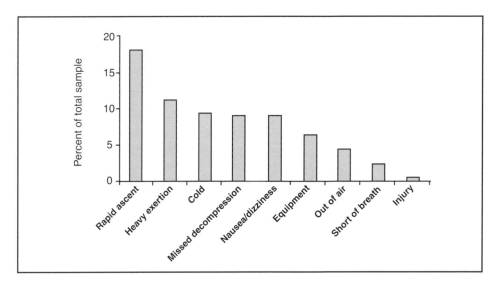

FIGURE 1.3 Frequency of reported problems during dives.
Reprinted with permission of Divers Alert Network.

even diving with experienced partners can be your ticket to safely enjoying something new and rewarding.

When you go to a new dive location, make your first dive in a very shallow, protected area. This will help to reacquaint you with diving skills that may have gotten a bit rusty and allow you to take small, incremental steps into the water. Proceeding with caution is far better than having to manage the emotional stress of having sucked up your entire air supply after looking down into the maw of a deep, open-ocean drop-off for the first time. This type of difficulty can happen even to divers who have been certified for many years but lack recent experience. If they have made dives in the same location under essentially the same conditions for years, they may not have gained the broad range of experience necessary to dive safely in a variety of diving environments.

What some people call a diver's comfort zone, we like to call a *personal safety envelope*. Training and certification, diving experience, equipment, and attitude all combine to define your personal safety envelope. All are equally and uniquely important in making your diving experiences safe and enjoyable. Before you push the edge of your envelope, make sure you have increased your skills so that you can successfully cope with all the demands of the dive.

Diving Environment

Every dive site is unique and presents it own set of challenges. Whether your dive site is freshwater or saltwater, warm or cold, you should know what to expect so that you can meet the challenges unique to that environment. Keep in mind that every site is dynamic, changing all the time. Just because it is calm and clear at the beginning of the dive doesn't mean it will be that way at the end. Many divers begin a dive under clear skies only to surface an hour later in a raging torrent! You must be prepared to handle everything that nature, or other divers, throw your way.

There are too many diving environments to list. They include everything from cold oceans to warm coral reefs (and wreck dives in either one), as well as drift diving with currents, deep shipwreck and wall dives, cold lakes, lakes at altitude, and freshwater rivers and springs. Each type of environment has more variables than we can discuss adequately in this book, and each site has its own unique features. If possible, get a dive site orientation from local divers or a local dive center. In each of the possible dive environments, you must be prepared to cope with temperature variations; thermoclines; surface and underwater currents, including surge, waves, and surf; changes in visibility; and aquatic life.

As you progress through your training and gain experience as an open-water diver, you are preparing yourself for the future. No two dive sites are alike, just as no two places on the surface are alike. Each site presents its own benefits and requires different approaches in terms of technique and safety.

◼ Orr's Safety Stop: Marine Life

Even though marine life is rarely a real threat to divers, it's always better to know what to expect in advance than to be surprised. On one particularly memorable trip to the shipwrecks off the North Carolina coast, I was able to observe the looks on the faces of some freshwater divers from Ohio as they encountered schooling sand tiger sharks for the first time. Although the sharks did not present much of a threat, they certainly did increase the divers' air consumption that day because of their menacing look.

Dive Planning

The old adage "Plan your dive and dive your plan" has been used since the inception of the sport. Some level of planning should be an integral part of every diving excursion, even if you have gone diving in that same location numerous times. You and your dive partner should go over all the details of the dive before heading out.

Because communication underwater is severely limited, even with the use of recognized hand signals or slates, you and your dive partner should discuss everything possible prior to commencing the dive, including the following:

- Planned bottom time
- Planned maximum depth
- Direction or course of travel
- Your individual and combined objectives
- Anything else that should be clearly understood before getting in the water, such as the dive signals you'll use for communication

When planning your dive, think about problems that could occur and prepare yourself for them. Remember that after a particularly deep or long dive, you may be tired. If you are caught in an unexpected current, you have to be ready to handle it. If the visibility at the dive site is not what you expected and you aren't prepared for low visibility, you need to have a contingency plan, which may include the use of a buddy line, or be prepared to abort the dive.

Even if you and your dive buddy have spent many hours diving together in a variety of diving environments, it is still a good idea to make sure that you both have the same understanding of the upcoming dive. Each of you should agree on the parameters of the dive so that the experience doesn't turn into an exercise in frustration and wild hand gesturing. Never take for granted that your diving partner understands everything. Communicate on the surface so that you don't have to communicate everything underwater. A safe and enjoyable dive is the result of a series of coordinated and well-communicated steps. Anything less will put you, and quite possibly your friendship, at risk.

If you happen to be a traveling diver and do not have the luxury of having your favorite dive partner with you, that, in and of itself, can present its own set of stressors and safety issues. Few things are more upsetting and possibly dangerous for traveling divers than to be assigned a buddy whose experience and skills, and perhaps personality and attitude, do not complement their own.

When traveling, you may want to spend some time trying to locate a compatible diving companion on your own rather than risk the luck of the draw or the process of being assigned a partner by the local dive guide. No one wants to relive the embarrassment of being the last one picked for the team in gym class. And dive guides do not necessarily match divers with the same or compatible skill levels, whether or not they strive to do so. It is not uncommon for novice divers to be assigned to instructors traveling alone, and for less experienced divers to be matched with those who are more experienced.

Keep in mind that when it comes to your safety and the safety of others, you can always say no. Far too often a diver will utter what may be the most dangerous words one diver can say to another: "Don't worry; I will take care of you." That phrase implies that one of the two is, for whatever reason, not as qualified, experienced, or skilled as the other. Too often an overconfident diver will make such a statement to an unwitting companion to convince him or her to agree to an excursion into a cave or wreck that may result in the tragic death of one or both of them. A safe diving experience should involve two equally trained and qualified partners who are compatible in terms of skills, training, and attitude. Anything short of that increases the risk dramatically.

© Bruce Coleman

Ensure dive safety and enjoyment by thoroughly planning your dives with your buddy.

Predive Safety Checks

Predive safety practices begin when the divers prepare their equipment and should include familiarization with all the equipment used by those they will be diving with. This process continues throughout equipment assembly and configuration. Divers should also be familiar with each diver's weighting system and how weights are jettisoned.

If you are preparing to dive from a boat for the first time, or if you are subject to motion sickness, you should prepare your equipment before the dive boat leaves the dock. Trying to configure your equipment on a moving vessel may create a situation that taxes even the strongest stomach. A touch of *mal de mer* may also cause you not to be as attentive or observant as you would otherwise be, increasing the possibility that equipment preparation errors go uncorrected. You cannot assume that the divemaster or boat captain will correct configuration errors or make sure that your air is on before you enter the water.

Teamwork in preparing equipment is an important safety consideration. Assembling and configuring your equipment as a team or buddy pair is a positive way of familiarizing yourself with your buddy's equipment. At the same time, it offers an opportunity to recognize possible assembly or configuration errors. If your diving partner is doing something different from you, stop and ask; it may be an indication that one of you has made an error that can have disastrous consequences later on. This philosophy should extend to others in your diving party and on your dive boat. If you see another diver with an unusual configuration or notice anything that may present a problem, you should bring it to the attention of the diver or the dive leader. After all, a crisis in the water could involve you or other nearby divers and could be catastrophic for more than just the diver with the equipment problem. You may not be your "brother's keeper," but you surely don't want your brother putting you at risk on a dive.

Divers who prepare their equipment together can identify and prevent many errors that could lead to problems in the water. In some ways, this is a logical and appropriate expansion of the buddy concept. The experiences and knowledge you gain through interacting with others during the out-of-water portion of the dive outing will help expand your knowledge and make you a better diver. The exchange of ideas, experiences, and even the ever-present sea stories (some of which may even be true) add to the experience of diving. Don't miss out on opportunities to learn something while talking with fellow divers before and after the dive. Other divers may be a valuable source of information about dive locations, equipment use, configurations, and recent developments.

Simply observing other divers on the same dive boat or at the same dive site can also be helpful. You might learn new ways of using a piece of equipment that will improve your diving safety, or you may find a way to correct a potentially dangerous equipment preparation error. If you see something that looks out of the ordinary, a casual conversation addressing what you have seen may give you some new ideas or provide an opportunity to help create a safer or more enjoyable diving experience for someone else. Another way to handle a potentially dangerous situation would be to quietly bring it to the attention of the dive guide, divemaster, or boat captain and let that person determine whether or how the situation should be dealt with.

The time prior to beginning the dive can also be used to discuss with your diving partner how either of you would handle potential emergency situations such as being low on air, being out of air, or violating any critical aspect of your dive plan. This is especially important if you have limited experience with your diving partner. Considering the fact that not all approaches to diving emergencies are universally accepted and that some divers develop individual or pet procedures and practices, a few well-spent minutes can make recognizing and managing emergency situations during the dive less traumatic and can increase the likelihood of a positive outcome. This seems to be especially true for hand signals. It's not uncommon for hand signals to cause confusion. For example, if a diver were to use an unusual signal such as holding both hands at his throat, commonly used to indicate choking, to represent being low on air, a new buddy might assume that his partner was in serious trouble and immediately bring him to the surface to render aid. Creative yet unintelligible hand gestures can leave even the most experienced diver clueless and can leave a diver in distress waiting for a critical response. Figure 1.4 displays the common hand signals used by divers.

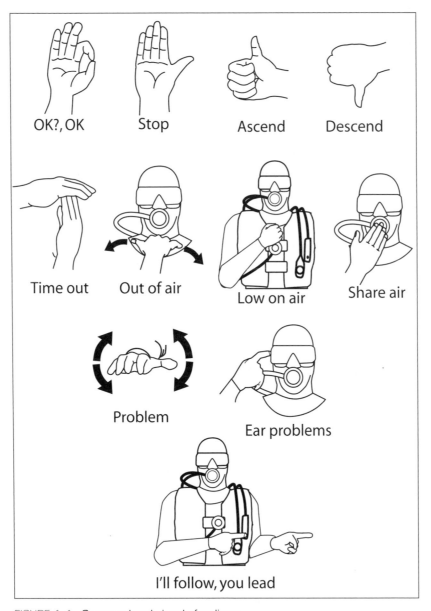

FIGURE 1.4 Common hand signals for divers.

Once you and your diving partner have prepared and configured your equipment properly, are well versed on the dive plan and each other, and are ready to don your equipment, teamwork is again a good idea. Helping each other put on equipment allows you to locate and correct twisted straps, reposition hoses or gauges that may be under other pieces of equipment, and make sure everything is assembled and configured correctly. If you are diving for the first time from a stable platform such as the shore or a boat deck, take a few minutes to review and reinforce critical emergency skills such as the exchange of air. Providing air in an underwater emergency involves some pretty complex psychomotor skills. It is essential that you practice these skills periodically so that you can use them quickly and effectively in an emergency. If the dive site has the potential for low visibility, practice some skills and locate critical equipment systems with your eyes closed. Such preparatory drills can come in handy when you least expect them to.

Entry Safety Tips

In open water it's best to have an uninterrupted supply of air through your regulator from the time you near the entry point until you are safely back on shore or aboard the dive boat. Anything less than that puts you at risk of unexpectedly aspirating water. Rocking and crowded boat decks and dive platforms can cause you to fall or be pushed into the water, or experience other types of problems through no fault of your own. It is safer to have the regulator rather than the snorkel in your mouth under such circumstances, because only the regulator will provide uninterrupted air when your head is more than 18 inches (46 centimeters) underwater. Additionally, with the regulator in your mouth, you'll be prepared to assist others if needed. You don't want to waste valuable time scrambling around trying to switch from snorkel to regulator when your partner or another nearby diver is in need of help.

Many divers automatically put the snorkel in their mouth before entering the water and immediately after surfacing from the dive. This could be a carry-over from having had a limited air supply and possibly running out during pool training exercises as students. A variation of Murphy's Law applied to diving physics dictates that waves will always be at least 1 inch (2.5 centimeters) higher than the length of any snorkel. The snorkel, traditionally worn attached to the mask, may create a safety hazard or annoyance when diving in currents. The snorkel can spin like a propeller or pull at the mask. Under these conditions, or in environments where wearing a snorkel is impractical (such as caves, or other overhead environments), you may want to carry a snorkel in a pocket or goody bag, or use a collapsible snorkel placed in the pocket of your buoyancy compensation device (BCD).

Donning your fins before initiating the dive can also be problematic. A good time to do so is just prior to entry. When entering the water from shore, carry your fins into the shallow water and work with your buddy to put them on. Trying to walk even short distances with fins on a slippery and moving deck or to navigate around rocks or other divers is difficult at best and a potential formula for disaster.

As you and your buddy prepare to move to the entry point, you can identify and practice emergency procedures such as air-sharing techniques. If conditions permit, each of you can also go through the location of your weights and simulate jettisoning them. Just as important, but not equipment related, is the review of critical hand signals and of the dive plan. Once this is done, both of you should conduct a complete head-to-toe (or mask-strap-to-fin-strap) buddy check (see figure 1.5) and correct any potential problems.

Just prior to the actual entry, if conditions and the proximity of your buddy permit, do another brief head-to-toe equipment check and take care of any last-minute issues such as hair in the mask seal or twisted straps. It is better to take the time to deal with these issues while still on the boat or shore than to have to do it in the water.

FIGURE 1.5 Dive buddies should always check each other's gear to make sure they are both ready to dive.

Postentry Check

Once in the water, do a quick visual equipment check of your own equipment. Your ability to completely scan your own equipment is limited, though, so you must rely on your buddy to make sure nothing has been displaced by the entry (see figure 1.6). Pay special attention to the mask, fins, weight belt or weighting system, valve/regulator, and hose connections. Predive and postentry routines have been called different things by different people and groups. The cave and

FIGURE 1.6 Practice air-sharing and other emergency drills frequently, and always perform a quick postentry check before beginning the dive.

technical diving communities call them *safety drills* or *S drills* and generally focus on air-sharing skills. These drills enable divers to become familiar with each other's air-sharing techniques and equipment. Predive safety drills should be more comprehensive than the postentry check and should be incorporated into the overall predive preparation process.

If the possibility exists for low-visibility conditions and the situation permits you to do so safely, practice safety skills with your eyes closed. You should practice safety skills at the beginning of each diving day, but it is especially important to do them if you will be diving with a new partner or have not had any recent diving activity, ideally in a controlled environment under the supervision of an instructor. Practice reinforces complex skills and helps to maintain proficiency. Time spent practicing emergency skills and doing the appropriate safety checks is well spent and will increase your confidence that, in the unlikely event of an emergency situation, the outcome will be successful.

Safety Procedures for the Dive

Once you are ready to descend and have given and received the appropriate OK signal from the dive leader and your buddy, the dive begins. If there is a strong current or wave action, if you suspect that you may have difficulties during descent, or if you are apprehensive in any way, use the anchor line or a descent line. A descent line (see figure 1.7) leading to the bottom will help you maintain your position relative to the intended dive site and can give you great comfort if you have little or no bottom reference during the descent. For a more comprehensive discussion of descent lines, see chapter 12, Currents and Dams. An anchored boat may also have a *swim line* that leads from the swim platform or entry platform to the anchor line or descent line. Once you enter the water, grab the swim line and move out of the way to allow your buddy to enter. Once you and your diving partner are ready, you can use the swim line to help pull yourself to the anchor line for your descent. Using the swim line will also help you on your return to the dive platform at the end of the dive.

FIGURE 1.7 Descending to a dive site along a line aids divers when a current is present or when visibility is reduced and might cause diver disorientation.

Always be aware of what is happening to you and your partner during the dive so that you can modify your dive plan to cope with anything that might otherwise compromise your safety or that of your diving partner. A plan for making adjustments during the dive should have been part of your predive discussion. Awareness of yourself, your partner, and the factors that could increase your risk and compromise your safety—knowing that the water was cold and you were chilled during the dive or that you worked a little harder than usual, for example—may call for you to modify your dive, reduce your bottom time, or add time to your safety stop.

Buddies should always agree prior to the dive that either member of the pair can *call the dive*, (that is, give the thumbs-up signal terminating the dive) at any time for any reason. This should be an accepted practice and an integral part of any safety-conscious dive partnership. Should either partner decide that something is wrong, that partner must be able to freely and without any recrimination give the signal to terminate the dive. At that time, both divers should initiate the previously agreed-on surfacing procedure. Unless the situation dictates otherwise, a safety stop is always a good idea.

Once the appropriate depth is achieved, both partners should be aware of their location relative to the other and to the anchor line, descent line, or exit point. It is best to move at the pace of the slower diver. Never expect someone to catch up to you. A diver who is having difficulty coping with the physical rigors of the dive increases the risk to both partners. Once you have achieved your shared objectives during the dive (which could simply be to have the greatest time of your life!) or reached the limits of your dive plan, you begin your ascent.

Current philosophy dictates that all dives, even those well within the no-stop limits of tables and computers, should include a controlled ascent (dictated by the diver's computer, tables, or personal or training philosophy) and a safety stop. Newly published research recommends slower ascent rates (slower than 60 feet, or 18.2 meters, per minute according to most tables) possibly coupled with multiple safety stops. Reading the available data published by the training associations and DAN is a good way to become familiar with the latest information on ascent protocols.

Safety stops provide an opportunity for you to make sure that your equipment is in order and that you slow your ascent before you make the final ascent to the surface—and place yourself in the area in the water column where the pressure change is the greatest. Take advantage of the opportunity. The real purpose of the safety stop, however, is to allow your body to continue to off-gas accumulated nitrogen before you return to surface pressures. Current recommendations for safety stop procedures vary slightly, but generally they recommend stopping your ascent between 15 and 20 feet (4.6 and 6 meters) for three to five minutes. This simple pause in your dive is not a required decompression stop. In an emergency, you can skip a safety stop and ascend directly to the surface. A decompression stop, on the other hand, is a planned and required stop based on the dive profile. Decompression stops are essential because they give your body time to remove excess nitrogen.

Depending on your dive location, the dive boat may lower a bar underwater at a predetermined depth—15 to 20 feet (4.6 to 6 meters)—for you to hold onto while completing your stop (see figure 1.8). This makes it easier to maintain a consistent depth if there are currents or wave action. It also provides room for more divers than a spot on an anchor line does. On a shore dive, you can usually rest on the bottom at about 15 to 20 feet (4.6 to 6 meters) outside the surf zone. In many quarries and lakes, divers frequently have rocks or other underwater features they use as points for safety stops. Whatever the plan, always be prepared to reduce bottom time or to adjust your ascent rate or safety stops in order to cope with a real or suspected increase in risk.

FIGURE 1.8 A bar suspended beneath the dive boat can make it easier to complete a safety stop at dive sites where there are currents or wave action. Safety stops allow divers to off-gas accumulated nitrogen and to slow their ascent.

Postdive Follow-Up

When back on board the boat or at the staging area on shore, you and your diving partner can help one another remove your equipment. Once the equipment has been removed and everything is either reconfigured for another dive or ready to be put away for the trek home, talk about the dive with your partner. This is a great opportunity to identify and discuss anything you could do better the next time or to reinforce new and improved skills or techniques. This is especially true if something, positive or negative, occurred that had never happened before. Because every dive is a unique experience in some way, treat it as an opportunity to learn. You will both be better divers for it. After all, diving, like life, is an experience best shared.

Equipment Use and Maintenance

Advances in the design of modern scuba dive equipment have virtually eliminated the possibility of equipment failure. Problems with equipment are usually caused by a lack of regular maintenance or self-maintenance or by the use of unfamiliar equipment, equipment the diver is not qualified to use, or equipment that isn't the correct size or configuration. Dive equipment, like any other tool, must be used appropriately. Using the wrong tool for the wrong job can only increase risk.

When selecting dive equipment, always consider that it is life-support equipment. Don't take shortcuts or try to make do with an item that isn't functioning properly. Use the appropriate equipment for the dive environment. Always follow the manufacturer's guidelines for maintenance, and have all equipment inspected annually by a trained and certified technician.

Rarely are dive equipment problems the direct cause of dive accidents. They can, however, increase a diver's stress in the water. The combination of a fogging mask, a leaking buoyancy compensation device (BCD) that creates buoyancy problems, and an entanglement may be more than a diver can handle, taking him from calm but annoyed to panicked and in trouble in a heartbeat. Simply caring for dive gear—your life-support equipment—is the surest way to avoid problems.

If equipment problems do occur, you need to be prepared and ready to take care of yourself or to assist a buddy in distress. Identifying and resolving a problem before it results in a more serious situation can turn a potential disaster into a simple aborted dive with no major consequences. Remember that any diver can call any dive, at any time, for any reason. Equipment problems that compromise a diver's safety are certainly reason enough to abort a dive.

Even with the proper training and experience, you must have the appropriate equipment for the dive situation or you will quickly get into trouble. Like diving in different environments, changing equipment can present some significant safety concerns. Because alternative, and sometimes radically different, equipment designs may require new or modified skill sets, you must gain experience with new equipment before using it in anything but the most benign open-water or confined water situation. Innumerable cases in the DAN accident data involve divers who used new equipment for the first time in the open water with disastrous results. David Colvard, MD, and noted diving psychologist Lynn Colvard, PhD, (2003) conducted research on diver panic; they identified "too many firsts" as a significant factor in increasing the risks involved in scuba diving.

That new BCD design, that new drysuit, even that new mask and fins may present you with challenges you have not experienced before. Even if you have the right equipment, you need to configure it appropriately to respond to the demands of the dive, including all possible emergency contingencies. You must also know your buddy's equipment as well as your own. If you want to enjoy the dive and successfully build on or expand your diving repertoire, gain some experience and confidence with your equipment in a pool or confined water, or in a course taught and supervised by a dive professional, before putting yourself and your diving companions at risk.

Masks

Masks, obviously, are essential pieces of equipment. They are made from silicone with soft, flexible skirts and straps (see figure 2.1). The maintenance for

FIGURE 2.1 Mask styles vary, but all masks require proper care after a dive.

them is pretty simple. Don't just throw them into your dive bag or bury them with the rest of your dive equipment, however. Heavy equipment, weights, or regulators can crack faceplates or break the buckles that hold straps in place. Following a dive, make sure to thoroughly rinse salt and dirt from your mask and put the mask in a protective storage container. Contact with other equipment, expecially items made of neoprene, can discolor clear silicone.

Common mask problems include a broken strap or hair in the seal causing water leakage. Worn-out or cracked mask straps may break, causing a dive mask to come loose and flood during a dive. An unexpected mask flood can certainly be an annoyance but may also lead to panic, causing a diver who is not prepared for the sudden inrush of water to escape to the surface. Despite proper care, because diving may involve limited visibility and the proximity of objects and other divers, the possibility always exists that a diver's mask will be accidentally flooded during a dive.

An experienced and qualified diver should be able to treat a mask flooding as a minor inconvenience and to replace and clear the mask without serious concern. This is especially true when the diver is involved in an emergency situation. If, in the midst of providing assistance to a diver in distress, the rescuer's mask accidentally floods and she must focus on her own survival, a potential rescue can turn into a tragedy for the diver as well as the rescuer.

For all of the preceding reasons, divers should practice all skills with and without their masks. Diver training should include exercises that clearly demonstrate that a diver can do everything without relying on the mask being in place and free of water. That includes all emergency scenarios, including providing assistance to an out-of-air diver. Some of the exercises can be as simple as clearing the mask without the use of the hands. This is important if your hands are needed for something essential such as helping a diver in distress. You should not need to stop what you are doing or reduce your control of the situation just to clear your mask.

A good training exercise involves having divers flood their masks and hold their hands out to their sides while looking up and rocking their heads back and forth and exhaling through their noses. This relatively simple exercise can be accomplished by divers at any level. Divers should also spend time regularly practicing, without their masks, breathing through their mouths and not holding their noses while their faces are submerged. This can be done in a pool or confined open-water setting prior to the start of a day's diving. Divers can even practice the skill with a snorkel in a bathtub or sink.

Exposure Suits

Water pulls heat away from our bodies more than 20 times faster than air does. Without exposure suits, such as dive skins, wetsuits, or drysuits (see figure 2.2), we could not enjoy the underwater world comfortably. In warm waters, dive skins provide some thermal protection as well as protection from sharp coral, barnacles, and stinging animals. Wetsuits and dive skins are simple pieces of equipment that need only the most basic cleaning and maintenance. Drysuits, on the other hand, need special care and maintenance to keep them functioning correctly as well as special training in their use. Once you determine which type of exposure protection you will need, based on the conditions of the dive, be sure to get the proper fit. Getting cold and uncomfortable on a dive can do more than decrease your enjoyment of the dive, it can increase your risk of accident or injury.

Dive Skins Dive skins are designed to provide limited thermal protection and keep the diver safe from jellyfish stings and abrasions from coral. They are typically made from a stretchy fabric and are designed to fit snugly. Many divers wear a dive skin under their wetsuit to make donning the wetsuit easier. To keep your dive skin in good shape, rinse it thoroughly after each dive, paying careful attention to the zipper and removing salt or grime that could build up there and foul its operation. You can also use wax or another lubricant on the zipper to help maintain easy zipping. Be sure that it is protected from abrasions or damage from heavy weights or other dive equipment, so it won't get torn.

Wetsuits Today's wetsuits come in a variety of thickness from 1/4 inch (3 mm) to 1/2 inch (7 mm), with variations in between, and feature different thicknesses on the body trunk than on the arms and legs. They come in assorted configurations, such as one-piece, back-zip suits; two-piece suits; shorties; and farmer johns. Talk to local divers, your instructor, and the staff at the local dive center for recommendations about appropriate protection for your diving environment.

FIGURE 2.2   Dive skins, wetsuits, and drysuits provide divers with protection from the elements.

A wetsuit should be snug but should not restrict movement or breathing. A wetsuit should be tight enough to reduce water circulation as much as possible, but loose enough to allow the diver to pull the suit on. Wetsuits should allow some water inside, where the body warms it, but should not allow continuous flow of water into and out of the suit. If the suit continuously allows water in and out, the body is continuously losing heat to the flow of water. Such a suit may keep you warmer than no suit, but you'll still lose body heat. With repeated use, and repeated expansion and contraction of the neoprene, a wetsuit may lose its thermal ability as the closed cells in the foam get compressed. The longevity of a wetsuit depends on how many dives you make and how well you care for it.

Drysuits Like any other piece of diving equipment, drysuits are tools that improve diving comfort and efficiency. They do, however, require quite a bit more care and preparation than other forms of exposure protection. Like many other types of equipment, drysuits require training in their use. Even experienced divers have gotten themselves in trouble by using drysuits either improperly or without appropriate training. Lost weights or the overinflation of a suit can cause a radical buoyancy shift and result in a rapid and uncontrolled ascent.

If you find yourself in an uncontrolled ascent while wearing a drysuit, you can open a wrist or a neck seal to vent excess buoyancy. Often, simply raising an arm straight up will allow air to vent through the cuff. You should also flare your arms and legs to slow your ascent and attempt to use the exhaust valve. By spreading out your arms, legs, and fins, you are increasing your surface area, creating greater drag and significantly slowing your ascent.

There are many different types of drysuits, from crushed neoprene to shell suits. Each comes with its own special properties and requires special instruction. A complete discussion of drysuits is beyond the scope of this chapter. You must pay particular attention to the drysuit zipper. This is the most expensive and most fragile part of the suit. You must apply wax or another lubricant recommended by the manufacturer to the zipper to keep it moving freely and must be careful not to crease it when you fold the suit for storage. Also, take great care with the neck and wrist seals of the suit. These should be replaced if worn or torn. A flooded drysuit, which can lead to a catastrophic cascade of events, generally results from a poorly maintained zipper, a split cuff or neck seal, leaking valves, or a diver who doesn't know how to prepare it for a dive. Wear an appropriate undergarment under your drysuit; the drysuit keeps you dry, but the undergarment keeps you warm.

Fins

Fins are relatively simple devices: They strap to your feet with either rubber or wire-assisted straps and help you move through the water. However, there are many styles to choose from. Divers who dive in warm water all the time may

FIGURE 2.3 The variety of available fin types allows divers to select the type best suited to the diving situation and to their personal preference.

choose full-foot fins worn without boots. Divers who use wetsuits or drysuits typically choose open-heel fins so that they can wear boots.

Different styles of fins are appropriate for different swimming styles and various diving circumstances (see figure 2.3). Freedivers, who want a lot of propulsion with a minimum of movement, typically use fins with very long blades. Scuba divers can choose fins with short blades, longer blades, stiff blades, or blades that are more flexible. There are even fins with split blades. Individual preference will affect your choice of fins. You should discuss your options with your dive instructor or local dive center and practice with an assortment of fin types, if possible, before making a choice. Don't use a new or different style on a stressful or physically demanding dive without prior practice.

If you typically dive in low-visibility conditions or often lead dives in which other divers follow you, try fins with bright colors. Sometimes all another diver can see is that bright color on your fins.

Fins should fit snugly, but should not be so tight that they are uncomfortable. Many times, divers experience feelings of numbness, tingling, or pain in their feet simply because their fins are too tight. This is commonly referred to as fin-foot. Using fins that are the wrong size or that have poorly maintained straps can result in losing a fin or getting foot cramps. Although a foot or calf cramp can be managed during a dive by stopping, grabbing the fin tip, and then stretching the foot or leg out, either problem can cause a diver to lose propulsion and get in trouble, especially when swimming in a current or trying to keep up with other divers.

If you lose and cannot relocate a fin while you are swimming, you can cross your legs to propel yourself through the water with one fin. You will be somewhat less effective using this technique, but you will still be able to make good headway. You should immediately signal your buddy and abort the dive, however. If you lose both fins, you can use a scissor kick or breaststroke to make your way through the water, but there should be no question: Abort the dive! You can also use your BCD to create sufficient positive buoyancy for a controlled ascent to the surface.

Buoyancy Compensation Devices

Buoyancy compensation devices (BCDs) fall into two basic categories: jacket style and back-inflation style (see figure 2.4), although there are numerous variations within those categories. All BCDs provide positive buoyancy on the surface, allow you to achieve neutral buoyancy while underwater, and help keep the rest of your equipment together (your tank on your back and your regulator in your mouth).

Your BCD should fit the type of diving you will be doing, and it should fit your body well. If you have to let the adjustment straps all the way out, or cinch them all the way in to make the BCD fit, the device probably isn't the correct size for you. If you plan to do a lot of underwater photography or cave and wreck penetration, a back-inflation-style BCD commonly referred to in cave diving circles as *wings*, is probably appropriate. However, this style may

FIGURE 2.4 Variations on two basic BCD designs meet the needs of divers with many different diving styles and purposes.

not be appropriate or necessary if you are just diving to have fun in the open water. Although they make it easier to swim horizontally through the water, when fully inflated wings may tend to force your face into the water when you are on the surface. Obviously, this can be an uncomfortable feeling for a novice diver. As with any piece of diving equipment, try out several styles and models of BCDs in a controlled environment to make sure you get one that is suited to you.

Problems with BCDs include a loss of buoyancy from holes or leaks and positive buoyancy issues caused by leaking air into the BCD from a poorly maintained power inflator. Air leaking into the BCD may result in an uncontrolled ascent. Once the diver is on the surface, a continuously inflating BCD can cause further problems by increasing pressure on the diver's chest and making breathing difficult. Another common BCD problem is the inflator hose or inflator connection leaking or popping off as a result of salt or sand buildup in either the hose or the connection. Loose straps or releases can cause cylinders to slip from the BCD during a dive. This can seriously compromise your safety, because a slipping cylinder can pull the regulator and power inflator away from you. Any of these problems can compromise your safety during a dive.

As with any other piece of diving equipment, you should have your BCD serviced regularly by a qualified service technician. Service should include a check of the power inflator as well as the dump valves and other working parts. The inspection should also include an evaluation of the straps and buckles.

Regulators

Scuba regulators are true life-support equipment (see figure 2.5). Divers rely on them to provide uninterrupted air (or gas) during the dive. If divers don't use

FIGURE 2.5   Scuba regulators are designed to deliver air or breathing gas at any depth. Specific designs have features that allow for variable breathing resistance and prevent cold-water freeze-up.

or maintain their regulators properly, the result can be catastrophic. Some of the problems with regulators include attaching them incorrectly to the scuba cylinder, having hoses coming from the wrong port, and split or broken bite tabs on mouthpieces.

As divers learn to scuba dive, they are taught that the primary second-stage regulator comes over the right shoulder and the alternate second-stage regulator comes underneath the right arm. The high-pressure hose and submersible pressure gauge (and possibly the instrument console) then come under the left arm, and the low-pressure inflator hose comes over the left shoulder. But if the first stage regulator is mounted on the scuba cylinder upside down, the hoses are not routed the correct way (see figure 2.6). The hoses can be twisted in the appropriate directions, but this may make them inaccessible or extremely difficult to use in an emergency. Obviously, this is a simple error to correct, but it commonly occurs when a diver has been away from the water for a long time or is using unfamiliar equipment. More often than not, another diver on the scene will notice this configuration error. Again, recent practice and a complete buddy check will prevent problems.

A more serious configuration error has the hoses coming from the incorrect outlet ports on the first stage regulator. Most modern regulators are designed so that the diver cannot confuse a high-pressure outlet with a low-pressure outlet. It is possible, however, to use the wrong outlet port, causing a hose to be oriented in the wrong direction when the regulator is mounted to the scuba cylinder.

In an underwater emergency, or when a diver is swimming against a current, a broken or torn bite tab can cause a serious problem. If the bite tab is already broken or torn and the diver bites the rest of the way through it, assuming he doesn't choke on the piece of rubber in his mouth, the diver can no longer

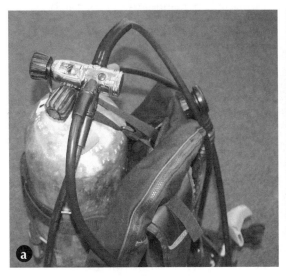 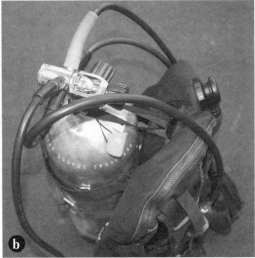

FIGURE 2.6 Regulator configurations: (a) proper configuration; (b) a common configuration error in which the first stage is attached to the cylinder yoke upside down, twisting the hoses. This error is often the result of the tank having been attached to the BCD backward.

effectively hold the regulator with his teeth. As he begins breathing harder and faster, trying to swim, he will be forced to struggle with the regulator as well. In and of itself, this is probably not serious, but it can be one more little problem that can cause a cascade of events leading to an accident. If the diver is already stressed, struggling with another equipment problem and a strong, unexpected current, having his regulator slip from his mouth may be all it takes to send him into panic.

Improper regulator maintenance has the potential to cause more serious problems. A leaking or broken second-stage diaphragm that isn't seating properly can allow water into the diver's mouth. With every inhalation, the regulator releases tiny water droplets or creates a fine mist that enters the diver's airway. This mist can cause the larynx to spasm (a condition known as a laryngospasm) potentially shutting off a diver's airway. If this condition isn't corrected and the larynx doesn't relax, the diver can literally suffocate. If your regulator leaks water into your mouth or throat, breathe slowly and use your tongue as a dam. You can also carefully use the purge button to provide additional air without forcing water into your airway. Keep the exhaust ports of your regulator pointed down to help prevent water from flowing inside the regulator, and abort the dive.

Another potentially serious regulator problem happens when, through improper maintenance or the formation of ice crystals, the regulator sticks in the open position and begins flowing air constantly. This is called a regulator free flow. Regulator freeze-up is also a significant concern for divers diving in cold water; many single-hose regulator designs may freeze up or free flow when temperatures are at or below 39 degrees F (4 degrees C). This phenomenon is related to the ambient temperature, the air or gas flow, the diver breathing rate, and possibly the presence of moisture in the breathing gas. Once free flow begins, if there is no way to isolate the malfunctioning regulator, the only alternative is to abort the dive.

At one time, a commonly held belief was that a diver could not breathe from a free-flowing regulator. During this period, a friend experienced a free flow while diving on a deep wreck in the Great Lakes. His buddy was not close by, so he jettisoned his free-flowing second stage and attempted an emergency ascent from 130 feet (40 meters). He lost his life because of an incorrect but well-circulated notion. Had he kept the free-flowing regulator in his mouth during his ascent, he may have been able to make it to the surface.

Fortunately, modern scuba regulators are designed to fail in the open position. This means they will start free flowing rather than shut off. You can breathe from a free-flowing regulator by allowing the excess air to vent from the sides of your mouth. Another option is to hold one bite tab between your teeth and allow the bite tab on the other side of the regulator to slip out of your mouth. This way, you can "sip" the air that comes out of the regulator as you need it and allow the excess air to vent out of your mouth. Breathe air as it flows by and use your tongue as a dam to keep any water out of your mouth and airway.

Although it is relatively simple to breathe from a free-flowing regulator, you cannot continue your dive. As soon as the free-flow develops, signal your buddy and make a controlled ascent to the surface. To prevent mechanical problems, have your scuba regulator serviced at least once a year before the diving season begins and choose a regulator design with features that resist freezing. If you are diving often, regularly leading divers, or working in the water, you may need to have your equipment serviced several times per year.

Finally, many a diver has jumped into the water only to find that her air is not turned on or not turned on completely. Often, divers will take a breath or two from their regulators when they put their equipment together and then turn the air off. Before you get in the water, breathe through your regulator while looking at the pressure gauge. If the needle fluctuates, your cylinder valve may be only partially turned on and must be adjusted to prevent catastrophic results once you are underwater.

Weight Belts

It may be hard to believe that one of the simplest pieces of dive equipment, one that needs little if any service, can still cause problems if it isn't used properly. But that is the case with the weight belt. If it is too long, you might be tempted to tuck in the open end or wrap it under your equipment. If the end of the strap is frayed, it may not fit through the buckle properly, or it may catch on the buckle when you attempt to release it and impair your ability to drop your weights in the event of an emergency.

Another type of problem occurs when the diver strings the belt through other equipment. Years ago, before the introduction of modern BCDs, divers used inflatable vests with crotch straps. On more than one occasion, divers got into trouble on the surface and attempted to jettison their weight belts as they had been taught, without realizing that they had buckled the crotch strap on their buoyancy device outside of the weight belt. When they flipped the buckle open to release the weights, the weights dropped only a few feet and hung between their legs from the crotch strap. As you can imagine, this made the situation even more dangerous. The divers were reluctant to reach down into the water to try and locate the problem or release their weight belts. It fell to observant buddies to intervene before the situation became more serious.

Weight belts can also cause problems if the quick release buckle is covered with a wetsuit or BCD, or slips around the body once the exposure suit compresses. To prevent the weight belt from shifting and to keep the release buckle in its proper place, position the weights in a traditional belt at, or slightly forward of, the hips. It is also a good idea to periodically check the location of the buckle during the dive to verify its proper positioning and to ensure that you, or a buddy or rescuer, can locate it quickly in an emergency.

Many divers today are using BCDs with integrated weight systems (see figure 2.7) featuring weight pockets built directly into the BCD to hold the weights.

FIGURE 2.7 BCDs with integrated weight systems are common today, but some divers opt for a more traditional weight belt.

Typically, they have easily identifiable release systems to allow for the release of the weights in the event of an emergency. As you prepare your equipment for the dive, you should check to make sure these quick release systems are set up and ready for use. If they are fouled, you won't be able to release your weights in an emergency. If they aren't configured properly and a weight, or an entire weight pocket, should fall out during the dive, you could easily find yourself in an uncontrolled ascent to the surface.

Regardless of the weight system you use, you must use the proper amount of weight. Being overweighted will cause you to struggle during the dive or swim in an awkward position, thereby expending more energy and using more air than necessary. Diving without enough weight can cause the same problems and the same drain on your energy and air. Being underweighted can also be dangerous at the end of the dive, because your scuba cylinder may be more buoyant, and the combined positive buoyancy can trigger an uncontrolled ascent, causing you to miss your safety stop.

Dive Tools

Dive knives or cutting tools that are designed to help a diver deal with potential entanglement problems can actually cause problems of their own if they are not configured properly. Divers often want to position dive knives on the outside of their legs to make them readily available. This position makes it easy for divers to get snagged on a fishing line, fishing net, or kelp while swimming. Knives or tools worn on the outside of the leg can also catch a weight belt that has been dropped. If you want to wear a dive knife or cutting tool on your leg, strap it to the inside of your calf. This will keep the tool accessible, but shield it and lessen the possibility of it getting caught on something in the water.

You should take the time to clean and dry your dive knife or cutting tool after every dive outing. With some basic maintenance, it will function well for years. You don't want to reach down for it only to find that it has become corroded beyond use.

3

Emergency Assistance Plans and Evacuation

As discussed briefly in chapter 1, Safety and Prevention, failure to fully prepare for a diving experience can have dramatic and potentially devastating consequences for you and your diving partners in the unlikely event of a diving emergency. Anytime you enjoy the outdoors, you must be prepared for the possibility of an injury or other situation that requires medical attention. Medical emergencies in diving can take many forms, ranging from minor problems that require simple first aid skills to more serious conditions that are unique to scuba diving and require treatment in specialized facilities. Because the most serious and potentially life-threatening injuries that result from an exposure to pressure while scuba diving may require specific first aid and treatment procedures, you must always know how to find a treatment facility that is capable of providing appropriate care for an injured diver. These specialized facilities must have a recompression chamber and staff who know the required regimen for treating decompression illness (DCI).

Preparing to manage a diving emergency is an essential part of dive planning. Dive accidents are rare, but you still need to be ready for one. A search for the most pristine or popular dive locations may take us to places where emergency medical services (EMS) are not readily available. We may be hours offshore on a boat, or on a secluded beach without lifeguards or nearby rescue personnel. Also, unfortunately, medical professionals frequently are not familiar with the unique nature of dive accidents and how to manage them. As a diver, you need to have a plan in place to handle an emergency. You also need to be prepared to evacuate an injured diver to a place that offers advanced and specialized medical care.

In the early years of recreational scuba diving, divers had to develop their own local or regional protocols for dealing with diving emergencies. Standard procedures involved basic life support (the ABCs: airway, breathing, and circulation), but unless you had the good fortune of diving in some of the more popular dive sites, locating the nearest appropriate treatment facility was left up to the individual diver or dive leader (divemaster or instructor). In some areas of the diving world, such as southern California, organized and highly trained groups were prepared to manage a diving emergency once notified. In some cases, help was as close as the nearest lifeguard tower; in others, resources were far more limited.

Prior to the creation of the diving emergency hotline at Divers Alert Network (DAN), most divers relied on a number for the U.S. Air Force Rescue Coordination Center in Texas, which was circulated around the instructor community. Because little else existed at the time, this number, known as the "LEO FAST" number, quickly became part of every diver and dive leader's emergency assistance plan (EAP). This number could be called in an emergency to help locate the nearest recompression chamber, many of which were located on military bases. Many divers also used the telephone number of the U.S. Navy Experimental Diving Unit. Even though both of these military units were as helpful as they could be, this system was far from perfect.

In 1980 the first diving emergency hotline for recreational divers came into existence with the creation of Divers Alert Network (DAN). Even though the experienced healthcare professionals at DAN are only a telephone call away for diving medical emergencies, it is still important to have an emergency assistance plan.

Emergency Assistance Plan

In an emergency, you don't have time to search for the answers to the questions that arise. You need to know the right phone numbers to call, the right things to say, and the right actions to take to care for an injured diver. This information constitutes your emergency assistance plan (EAP).

An EAP includes a list of phone numbers and contact information. It also includes an action plan for the specific location where you will be diving that tells you where to go and what to do in case of an emergency. An EAP is also a statement of preparedness: you've thought about what might happen and are ready to take action if necessary. Although much of the information on EAPs will be the same from one site to the next, each dive site will also have unique aspects that you need to be prepared to handle. To properly prepare an EAP, you need to take some time to think about the dive site. You'll need to determine what it would take to get a diver to qualified medical help, who would be available in the event of an emergency, and what you might need to make it all come together.

Putting together a detailed EAP may seem like quite a bit of work for something you will probably never need. Spending a few minutes gathering potentially lifesaving emergency information sure beats the alternative, however. EAPs can be as simple or as complex as the dive location and your personal safety requirements dictate. Regardless of the level of sophistication of your personal EAP, it should have the following characteristics:

- **It must be accessible.** Once you have prepared your plan, keep it in a place where you'll be able to find it quickly and where others will have easy access to it if you are underwater or you're the one who needs attention. The best method is to have multiple copies in several locations—in your equipment bag, in your vehicle, with your dry gear on the beach or on the boat. Make sure all your dive buddies know where it is and how to find it. If the only copy is in your car, then make sure everyone you're diving with knows how to find your keys.

- **It must be legible.** Make sure your plan is legible—easy to read and easy to understand. Don't use abbreviations known only to you or points of reference that others won't understand. Print it out on water-resistant paper so it will hold up to an accidental spill or being buried with wet dive equipment. Keep a copy of your EAP with your dry clothes and other gear. Using a dry bag or an extra-large zip-top bag to protect the contents from the ever-present moisture of a dive site is also a good idea.

- **It must be site specific and updated regularly.** Going more than a year without updating an EAP for a particular dive location is risky business. Don't bet your life on the fact that the contact information is still accurate without verifying it in some way. The potential for lasting injury from a delay should be motivation enough for you to keep all the information on your EAP current. Even if it has been only a short time since your last trip to a dive site, if you are unsure of the accuracy of the information, it is far better to be safe, and confirm or correct it, than sorry. Figure 3.1 shows a sample emergency assistance plan to help you get started preparing your own.

It is also important that you verify that you have a means of communication at the dive site. The current use of cell phones reduces the likelihood of this being a problem, unless your service provider does not have coverage in that particular location. Make sure your phone has a signal and is fully charged before relying on it during a diving excursion. If cell phone service is unavailable in the area where you will be diving, part of your predive protocol should be to locate the nearest public telephone and make sure that it is in working order. It is also a good idea to have a prepaid phone card that is acceptable in that region, especially if you are out of the country.

In some locations, Citizens' Band (CB) radios may still be a viable alternative method of contacting the local authorities in case of an emergency. Make sure you have the appropriate channel for the regional police, rescue squad, or EMS before relying on this method of emergency contact. On a dive boat with a VF marine radio, the usual emergency channel is channel 16, but you should confirm that that is the case in the area where you'll be diving.

When diving internationally, you can also acquire satellite phones that allow you to make calls from anywhere in the world. Although they are not practical for local calls, when you are diving in remote locations and need to be able to reach home or emergency help immediately, satellite phones are a tremendous help.

FIGURE 3.1
Sample Emergency Assistance Plan

Last updated _____

Dive site _____

Local emergency number (911)
or appropriate local contact _____

Location of the nearest pay phone or public phone _____

Location of the nearest cellular phone signal _____

Coast Guard radio frequency _____

Nearest medical facility	Directions from dive site
_____	_____
_____	_____
_____	_____
Phone ( ) _____	_____

See maps on reverse.

Emergency Procedures

☐ If a diver is lost, initiate emergency procedures.
☐ Determine the most appropriate search technique for the dive site.
☐ Secure necessary equipment.
☐ Recall other divers if there is an emergency.
☐ Organize rescue and first aid care and establish control.
☐ Alert rescue authorities.
☐ Prepare first aid equipment.
☐ Provide basic life support.

Basic Life Support

Assess scene safety. Remove the diver from the water if necessary, and ensure the safety of all rescuers.

1. Assess responsiveness. If the diver is unresponsive, immediately activate your emergency plan. Call for emergency medical services.

2. Open the airway and check for breathing.

3. If the diver is not breathing normally, deliver 2 rescue breaths.

4. Begin CPR. Immediately deliver 30 compressions followed by 2 breaths.

Provide emergency oxygen, if available, at the highest possible concentration using the most suitable delivery device.

From D. Orr and E. Douglas, 2007, *Scuba Diving Safety* (Champaign, IL: Human Kinetics).

If EMS help is not available, immediately transport the injured diver to the nearest emergency medical facility. Provide emergency department personnel with details concerning the accident and the contact information for DAN, included below.

Contact Information for DAN

919-684-8111 or 919-684-4DAN (4326) (Collect calls are accepted.)

Explain to the operator that you have a scuba diving emergency.

Personal Emergency Contact Information

Diver's name _____   Next of kin _____

Address   Address

_____   _____

_____   _____

_____   _____

Phone (   )_____   Phone (   )_____

Relevant Medical Information

Allergies _____

Conditions _____

Medications _____

Medical insurance information _____ Policy number _____

DAN member number _____

Family physician _____ Phone (   )_____

Additional relevant medical information _____

_____

_____

_____

_____

_____

(continued)

From D. Orr and E. Douglas, 2007, *Scuba Diving Safety* (Champaign, IL: Human Kinetics).

FIGURE 3.1 *(continued)*

Diving Emergency Information

Diver's name _____

Vital signs _____

Pulse _____ Respirations _____ Blood pressure _____

Signs or symptoms _____

_____

Allergies _____

_____

Medications _____

_____

Medical history _____

_____

Last meal or oral intake _____

Events leading to current situation _____

_____

Neurological assessment _____

_____

_____

_____

_____

Dive profile information _____

_____

_____

_____

_____

Emergency Medical Contact Information

Ideally, an injured diver should be transported by trained and qualified personnel. The emergency medical contact information in your EAP should include the telephone number of the local diving emergency response network; emergency medical services (EMS), including the rescue squad or ambulance service; and the Coast Guard as appropriate. Keep in mind that the local emergency response number is not always 911, especially if you are outside the United States. Although you should always contact DAN in the event of a dive emergency, in life-threatening situations, contact the local medical services first if at all possible. DAN's team of medical professionals will always refer you to the nearest medical facility for primary medical care and evaluation, and will work with that medical facility to ensure that the injured diver receives the proper care.

If a coordinated diving emergency response network exists in your area, you may be able to access trained professionals right at or near the dive site. Local divers and dive centers should be able to provide contact information for networks and rescue groups that operate in the area. If you are offshore, you may be able to use the appropriate radio frequency to contact the Coast Guard, access the local response network, or even contact DAN.

Location of the Nearest Medical Facility

Even though your EAP contains contact information for rescue and transport groups, it is also wise to include the location of the nearest available medical facility. Keep on hand the address of the nearest available medical facility and driving directions from the dive site to the facility, in case the circumstances dictate that the injured diver be taken to the medical facility in a private vehicle or boat. This, of course, is a method of last resort, to be used when no other medically supervised alternative exists, and it assumes that those responsible for the transport have all necessary first aid equipment and sufficient training to manage the injured diver.

Unless the driver is extremely familiar with the area, maps and directions are essential in this situation. Using the best technology available, GPS coordinates may help the rescuers locate the nearest medical facility, EMS, or Coast Guard unit. GPS technology can be found in handheld units or in specially equipped vehicles or vessels. Cell phones and GPS systems can be an extremely useful combination when a diver's health and welfare are in the balance. Many cell phones include their own GPS units that can help you find locations and help rescuers find you.

Basic First Aid Procedures

A comprehensive EAP should include some very basic first aid as a reminder to those responsible for managing the emergency.

Basic first aid is as follows:

- Establish and maintain the airway and breathing.
- Start CPR, if necessary.
- Place the injured diver in a recovery or supine (on back) position.
- Initiate and maintain 100 percent emergency oxygen first aid.

Create or obtain an emergency management form that has these instructions on it, so that it can serve as a reminder. As part of your emergency preparedness, make sure that everyone you dive with has the necessary training to initiate care for an injured diver and has taken a CPR refresher course recently. Typically, first aid and CPR certifications are good for about two years, although many people like to take a refresher course at the beginning of their dive season to ensure that their skills are sharp in case they need them. Having one or two people in a dive group with the appropriate training may not be enough. Everyone needs to be able to care for everyone else.

Diving Medicine Emergency Contact Information

DAN provides divers with a worldwide network of care in the event of an emergency. There are five affiliate DAN organizations:

- DAN America—covering North and South America as well as the Caribbean
- DAN Europe—covering all of Europe, the Middle East, and northern Africa
- DAN Southern Africa—covering sub-Saharan Africa
- DAN Japan
- DAN Asia-Pacific—covering the rest of Asia and the South Pacific

These DAN offices work together to care for divers injured anywhere in the world. It is important to know the DAN phone number for your region. If you don't know the local regional phone number while away on a dive vacation, you can always call your home DAN office collect and they will set the wheels in motion no matter where you are.

In the DAN America region, the emergency hotline phone number for diving emergencies is 919-684-4DAN. In Latin America, there are regional phone numbers. Throughout Europe, there are regional numbers to account for language variances. Figure 3.2 provides the numbers you'll need to contact DAN. Contacting any of these numbers will begin the process of coordinating care.

The DAN Diving Emergency Hotline is available 24 hours a day, 365 days a year to any diver who is in need of emergency assistance. DAN membership fees and donations help to support and maintain the hotline, which is available to all divers, members and nonmembers. Calling the DAN number will put you in contact with a trained and qualified diving medical professional who can assist you in managing a diving emergency. If you are a DAN member, diving and nondiving emergency contact information can be found on your DAN

FIGURE 3.2
DAN Phone Numbers for Diving Emergencies*

DAN America
1-919-684-8111
1-919-684-4326 (accepts collect calls)
DAN Latin America
1-919-684-9111 (accepts collect calls)

DAN Europe
39-06-4211-8685

DAN Japan
81-3-3812-4999

DAN Asia-Pacific
DES Australia
1-800-088-200 (within Australia)
61-8-8212-9242 (outside Australia)

DAN / DES New Zealand
0800-4DES111
Singapore Naval Medicine & Hyperbaric Center
67-58-1733
DAN Asia-Pacific – Philippines
02-632-1077
DAN Asia-Pacific – Malaysia
05-930-4114
DAN Asia-Pacific – Korea
82-010-4500-9113

DAN Southern Africa
0800-020111 (within South Africa)
27-11-254-1112 (outside South Africa)

*All phone numbers should be checked regularly to ensure correctness.

membership card. It is important to remember that this service is available to anyone who needs it, regardless of whether that person is a member.

Members have other benefits including DAN Travel Assist, which can be vital, especially in remote areas of the world where medically supervised evacuation to a specialized treatment facility may be needed for diving as well as nondiving injuries.

Recompression Information

If you are caring for a diver with signs of decompression illness, the only definitive care is recompression. At a recompression facility, the diver is returned to pressure and given 100 percent oxygen to help reduce the nitrogen dissolved in body tissues and eliminate bubbles from the body.

Once emergency medical assistance is underway, you can call DAN for assistance in locating the nearest recompression facility. If this is not housed at the medical facility where the local EMS will take the diver, the DAN medical professionals can liaise with the local medical staff to see that the diver is transferred to the nearest chamber. Local information regarding recompression facilities should not be relied on in an emergency situation; it should be considered secondary to information provided by DAN.

Although it's not a bad idea to have local recompression chamber information included in your EAP, you shouldn't take an injured diver directly to the chamber unless doing so is part of the regional protocol. The best course of action is to get the diver into the medical system at an emergency department so he can be properly evaluated and stabilized. Also, very few chambers are open and ready for patients 24 hours a day. By taking the diver directly to a chamber, you run the risk of the chamber being unable to help. The resulting delay could result in permanent injury or disability. In one case, a chamber listed on a diver's EAP had been dismantled and sold for scrap three years previously.

Personal Medical Information

If you have a medical condition or are taking medication that might in any way affect your treatment for a diving or nondiving emergency, note the condition or medication on your EAP. Having medical information on the form is especially important considering the fact that you could be incapacitated by the injury and unable to communicate. To be on the safe side, include copies of your primary health, as well as diving accident, insurance information in your EAP. As anyone who has ever been admitted to a medical facility knows, that information can certainly expedite your care.

Emergency Equipment

You never know when you will need to search for a diver in the water or initiate a rescue. To prepare for an emergency, you will need several pieces of equipment. Your EAP should include a checklist of emergency equipment. When you pack your equipment to head off to a dive site, verify that each of the following items is ready and available in the event of an emergency:

- Binoculars. These are useful for searching for a missing diver from the surface.
- Clipboard with pen and paper or a pencil and slate. You will often need to write down important information to communicate to emergency medical services—everything from a neurological assessment of the diver to the diver's pertinent medical history and dive profile.
- Surfboard or rescue board. If you need to swim out to a diver on the surface, a rescue board will give you stability and a place to provide care.
- Rescue float. When a diver is in trouble on the surface, helping him become positively buoyant on the surface may be all it takes to enable him to regain control.
- Rope or line. There are many different uses for lines on a boat and in a rescue. You may need to use a rope or line to search underwater for a missing diver, or to pull a diver to the boat. A rescue bag is especially useful in getting rope to a stranded diver on the surface.

- Circular sweep anchor. This type of anchor allows you to initiate an underwater search pattern from a fixed point.
- Diver compass. A diver compass can help you navigate search patterns.
- Marker buoys. You can use marker buoys to identify a search area, or the spot where a diver's buddy ascended to the surface.
- Flares. In case a boat is disabled or out of contact, you can use signal flares to attract help.
- Whistle. A whistle can quickly attract attention.
- Bullhorn. When coordinating a search in the water, you can use a bull-horn to communicate to divers on the surface and give them instructions on where to search.
- Radios. Two-way radios are useful for coordinating searches among boats, or alerting authorities as to the nature of the emergency. AM/FM radios are useful for monitoring changing weather conditions.
- Cell phone and location of a public phone. It is useful to note the location of public telephones because cell signals may not always reach your dive sites.
- Underwater recall system. Without some method to recall divers from the water, you may waste valuable time in an emergency waiting for all divers to return to the boat when you could be moving toward the shore and advanced medical care.

Emergency Evacuation

Having put your EAP into action by administering basic first aid, your next priority is getting the diver to further emergency assistance. When you contact help, declare that you have an emergency and state the nature of it, for example: "This is an emergency. I have a scuba diving accident onboard at . . . ." You should then provide information on your location (LORAN or GPS coordinates), your direction and distance from prominent landmarks, the environmental conditions, the status of the diver, and any unusual circumstances.

Although in most instances you will probably be able to make a call to local emergency medical services, or radio the Coast Guard, as you have outlined on your EAP, you may find yourself in a situation in which you must signal that help is needed. Several distress signals are internationally recognized and can be used if you are unable to contact help directly.

International Distress Signals

- Mayday (the spoken word)
- Gun or other explosive discharged at one-minute intervals
- Continuous sounding of a foghorn

- Rocket or shells throwing off red sparks
- SOS signal in Morse code (three long, three short, three long)
- Square flag with a ball above it or below
- Slowly and repeatedly raising and lowering arms outstretched to sides

Other Marine Distress Signals

- Inverted U.S. flag (United States)
- International orange cloth with a black square and ball on it (United States, Canada)
- Red cloth (Caribbean)
- Green fluorescent dye marker
- Flashes from a signal mirror
- Smoke from a signal fire (three fires in a triangle is a definite distress signal)

Depending on the nature of the emergency, the Coast Guard may decide to airlift the injured diver from the boat instead of waiting until the boat reaches shore. In making this determination, the Coast Guard will take all relevant factors into consideration, including transport times, sea conditions, and the medical condition of the injured diver. If the diver isn't stable, you may not be able to execute the transfer. If you are performing CPR, you should not attempt a transfer. The helicopter crew may not have the room or the training to perform CPR, and you can't interrupt it for the amount of time it will take to prepare for the lift and get the diver into the helicopter.

Because removing an injured diver from a dive boat on the open water is a dangerous and tricky maneuver, it is not undertaken lightly. If the Coast Guard is going to lift an injured diver from the deck of a dive boat, the boat crew and helicopter personnel must work together throughout the three main stages of the transfer.

1. Prepare for the Lift

There is a lot to do onboard the boat to prepare for the lift. A member of the boat crew should begin to prepare the boat by lowering all tall objects such as radar and fishing equipment. As the helicopter nears the boat, the force of the prop wash can lift large items and throw them around. All the divers on board can help by securing any loose objects; this includes everything from coats, hats, and towels to heavier items such as dive equipment bags.

The injured diver should wear a personal flotation device during the lift, regardless of how the crew plans to lift him off the boat—whether in a litter or with a harness (see figure 3.3). If at all possible, send along the emergency oxygen unit. The helicopter may not have one onboard. Also send along with the diver any information you recorded as part of the accident—whether the diver can communicate or not. This will include the diver's medical history, dive profile, and any findings from the neurological assessment you conducted as part of your examination. Send the diver's dive computer, if available, so the medical facility can determine the diving history. Finally, if possible, send the diver's buddy along. The buddy may also need recompression therapy, since the dive profiles for both partners would be similar, if not identical.

2. Communicate With the Helicopter

Bringing together a helicopter and a dive boat on the ocean is a tricky maneuver that requires careful execution. The captain of the boat and the flight crew of the helicopter need to communicate very carefully to make sure there are no misunderstandings.

During the actual lift, the pilot of the helicopter is in charge. The pilot will probably have more experience in coordinating a lift and will know what is needed to make it happen. Typically the boat should head into the wind at about 5 miles (8 kilometers) per hour to make the lift easier to manage—although the pilot will give the captain the actual course and speed. When everything is ready on the boat deck and the diver is prepared for the lift, the captain should alert the pilot and then allow the helicopter to approach the boat.

3. Complete the Lift

The helicopter propellers and the downwash of the wind generate a tremendous amount of static electricity. This electrical charge can injure a would-be rescuer on the boat. If a line is hanging from the basket stretcher being lowered from the helicopter, don't touch it. Allow the line or the basket itself to hit the deck of the boat before anyone touches it. This will discharge any built-up static electricity harmlessly into the boat and the water. Once the basket is down, load the diver as quickly as possible, but don't tie the basket down. Allow it to move around in case the pilot needs to move the helicopter.

After the lift has been completed, remember that the flight crew may not have much experience with injured divers. Remind the pilot of the need to fly as low as safely possible—preferably below 800 feet (243 meters) to avoid worsening the condition of the diver. DAN representatives may have already

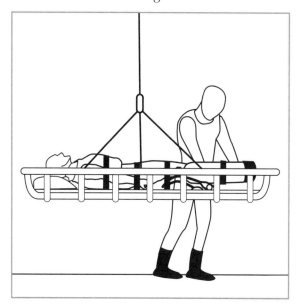

FIGURE 3.3 Secure the diver into the litter lowered from the helicopter. Include emergency oxygen equipment and other necessary information for the diver's treatment.

conveyed this information, but it is safest to remind them. If the diver has nitrogen bubbles in his body from the dive, an ascent to altitude may make these bubbles increase in size or cause more bubbles to form. You should also advise the helicopter crew to keep the diver on 100 percent oxygen, if they have their own unit or you were able to transfer yours with the diver, and to contact DAN for further guidance.

After you return to the dock following a dive emergency, maintain the diver's equipment in the condition it was found for future evaluation. Do not disassemble, reassemble, or inspect the equipment yourself. Leave that to the professionals, who will examine the equipment for any clues as to the factors that contributed to the incident. If you have not already done so, contact DAN to report the dive accident for inclusion into the accident and fatalities database.

4

Emergency Recognition and Prevention

Although diving is a fun and relatively safe sport, emergencies do occasionally occur. At any time you could find yourself in a situation in which you must act as a rescuer. Being aware of what is going on around you and being prepared may help you to avert a crisis before it happens. After all, part of what all divers do is problem solving. Each dive presents a unique set of circumstances. Safe, competent divers assess the circumstances and find ways, using their training and skills, to resolve the issues that arise. On the other hand, divers who lack essential skills and training may quickly find themselves in an emergency because they cannot cope with the challenges of a given situation.

You should develop the skills necessary to recognize potential problems before they escalate. This doesn't mean that you should be examining every diver around you and trying to figure out who is going to have trouble. But, with experience, you will begin to notice things that just don't seem right. Your attitude should be similar to that of an off-duty police officer scanning a crowd casually for trouble spots even when not responsible for crowd control. You don't have to be expecting a problem, but if one occurs, you should be able to pick up on it quickly and easily. Dive leaders often have this ability; they often find themselves organizing other divers above and below the water. Seasoned dive leaders are always ready to act if someone needs help.

A good way to learn from the mistakes of others is by talking with other divers about their experiences, reading about other divers' experiences in dive magazines, or reviewing the accident narratives in publications such as DAN's *Alert Diver* magazine or the *Report on Decompression Illness, Diving Fatalities and Project Dive Exploration*. Analyze the behaviors and actions of divers in these situations and compare it with your own. Make modifications in your own diving procedures as necessary to reduce risk and enhance your readiness to deal with problems.

The signs of emergencies are varied and can be subtle. They may be apparent before or during the dive. A diver's ego or peer pressure may cause him to disguise a problem, such as a lack of competence, inadequate experience, overconfidence, anxiety, illness, or distress. Such problems may show up on the boat before anyone gets in the water. All divers should adopt the credo of the cave and technical diving communities: *Any diver can call any dive for any reason at any time.* No questions are asked—and the credo applies before the dive even begins. All divers should agree to this as part of the predive briefing. If more divers felt comfortable not making a dive because it was beyond their experience, or they didn't feel well, or their karma was all wrong, or whatever, there would probably be fewer problems.

Surface Emergencies

A good place to start in recognizing problems at the surface is with the equipment. A diver, especially one with limited experience, who appears to be overequipped for the dive is a cause for concern. The diver may simply be behaving prudently, practicing or refreshing his skills with full cave equipment and double cylinders in a 30-foot lake before returning to an overhead environment. On the other hand, the diver may have brought more equipment than needed in attempt to compensate for some fear or deficiency.

You should also be aware of ineptness or errors in assembling equipment or getting into the water. Correcting errors is everyone's responsibility. Any indications of a lack of knowledge, nervousness, or repeated mistakes should raise concern and cause you or those in charge to closely observe or subtly inquire about diver's experience and qualifications for the upcoming dive.

Other problem signs may manifest psychologically. A normally talkative diver who is quiet and withdrawn just before making a dive might be experiencing predive anxiety. In another diver, being overly talkative may indicate stress. A change in the pitch of the diver's voice, incessant chattering and joking, and delaying getting ready may all indicate that something is not quite right. These signs may be difficult to evaluate because they require some knowledge of the diver's normal behavior. The traveling diver who is meeting a buddy for the first time at the dive boat may have difficulty reading the buddy's demeanor. Remember, you can call a dive at any time, even before it begins, or you can ask to dive with another diver or the divemaster.

After a diver is geared up and ready, there are additional signs to watch for. A diver who clearly doesn't understand the entry technique you are using, seems distracted, or forgets equipment and ignores instructions from the divemaster may be experiencing predive anxiety and may require some intervention or professional care beyond the scope of the standard dive-buddy relationship.

◼ Orr's Safety Stop: Experience and Credentials

One word of caution: When working as a team, make sure both divers are fully capable of preparing for the dive themselves. I get very nervous when a prospective buddy mimics everything I do. Early in my professional diving career, I managed a popular recreational dive site in the Midwest. One of my many roles included identifying anyone lacking the appropriate diving credentials.

One day, a diver who vehemently professed his diving experience but was unable to produce either verification of certification or a logbook was brought to me for an open-water evaluation. I had my suspicions from the beginning. He mimicked everything I did after I did it. Just prior to entering the water, I decided to see how far this would go. Sitting on the end of the dock alongside the diver, I spit into my mask to prevent fogging (this was long before commercial mask-clearing compounds), rinsed it out, and then donned the mask. He, of course, watched me and then followed suit. I then spit into my fins and rinsed them and put them on. He did the same. At that point I said, "Whoa. Hold on a minute!" He subsequently admitted that he was not certified after all. Thereafter, I made it a personal rule never to dive with divers who spit into their fins!

Dive leaders should take care not to spend all their time working with students and getting them ready and in the water, without taking time to prepare themselves properly for the dive. All good dive leaders understand that they lead—and dive—by example. This includes demonstrating all the rules that they establish and teach. There is no excuse for not following proper procedures. To prevent problems, dive leaders should either treat the entire group or class as a buddy, or delegate one member as their buddy, and follow all the predive checks that they require of their students.

Another indication that there may be a problem is when a diver fails to buddy up properly after entering the water, fails to check on a buddy, or fails to maintain appropriate buddy contact after the dive begins. A sure sign of a problem is a diver struggling to maintain surface orientation. The diver may begin *high-treading*, or struggling to keep his head above water, rather than relaxing and using his own equipment to help him (see figure 4.1). Divers should put sufficient air in their BCD to be slightly positively buoyant upon entry. Then when they are ready, they can simply dump the air from their BCD and begin their feet-first descent. Inexperienced or anxious divers may forget about the air in their BCD, begin a head-first surface dive, and find that they can't get to the bottom—at which point their orientation prevents them from dumping the air from their BCD.

FIGURE 4.1 High-treading is an indication that a diver is not using his equipment properly.

It can be helpful to advise anxious divers to look down in the water. A few seconds with their face down allows them to survey the bottom briefly and seems to have a calming effect on those with a bit of anxiety or nervousness. They are able to relax and allow their training to take hold. Other obvious indications of a problem include a diver crying for help, swimming with her arms up, using a whistle to attract attention, actively struggling, or appearing ill or unconscious.

Underwater Emergencies

Dive emergencies underwater happen for a number of reasons. Usually, however, they aren't catastrophic problems to begin with. Underwater emergencies typically start with a minor problem that escalates into a bigger one, as discussed earlier.

You should be constantly on the lookout for potential problem situations. Any deviation from good diving practice should be a signal that a problem situation exists or may develop later in the dive if circumstances don't improve. The deviation can be as simple as a change in a diver's body position or swimming orientation, indicating possible overweighting or some other problem. If you dive with someone regularly, any deviation from the person's normal habits should be cause for concern.

Adhering to proper dive procedure prevents problems. Although you will want to spend your time exploring reefs or wrecks or whatever you find underwater, remember to check your cylinder pressure and depth, as shown in figure 4.2, on a regular basis during your dive. If you are performing tasks such as underwater photography or feeling distracted during the dive and don't have an observant and watchful diving companion, you may forget about the basics and find yourself out of air while still underwater. Obviously, running out of air underwater is a formula for disaster. Divers may also forget to pay appropriate attention to their dive buddies. This can have serious consequences for both buddies if they should get separated and either one has a problem.

© Lynn Seldon

FIGURE 4.2   Keep close tabs on your air pressure while you are diving to avoid potential problems.

Factors that contribute to underwater problems include fatigue, heat or cold stress, equipment malfunction, a lack of recent familiarity with basic skills, and overconfidence. Divers get into trouble when they ascend rapidly, exceed the no-decompression limits of their dive computers or tables, or fail to follow appropriate decompression procedures. Divers also have difficulty when they underestimate environmental hazards such as tidal currents flowing through channels, rip currents and breaking waves, or the force of a current pushing them away from their dive platform or boat. Surface obstructions such as a kelp canopy, docks, piers, and vessels can cause problems for divers who ascend into them. The stress of trying to manage any of these difficulties can lead divers to make inappropriate decisions, such as trying to return underwater with a limited and possibly inadequate air supply.

Physiological Emergencies

Aside from the procedural problems that can cause emergencies during a dive, physiological issues can cause problems as well. Nitrogen narcosis is a physiological problem that can lead to poor decision making and carelessness on a deep dive. Another problem is nausea and vomiting caused by seasickness. Feeling ill can make divers less alert and inhibit their ability to effectively prepare for a dive or to manage problems if they arise. Other physiological problems that can lead to emergencies include disorientation and fatigue.

Nitrogen Narcosis

Nitrogen narcosis is a purely physiological reaction in the body to the nitrogen in one's breathing gas at depth. The actual mechanism is poorly understood, but as divers descend, nitrogen exerts a narcotic effect. Although symptoms can be felt earlier, most people regard nitrogen narcosis as a problem only on dives greater than 100 feet (30.4 meters) deep. It continues to increase with depth, making divers less likely to use good judgment the deeper they go.

The narcotic effect of nitrogen can lead to poor decision making, lack of self-control, and violations of dive plans. Divers have told stories of not realizing they were passing depths of 200 feet (60.8 meters) or more when they had planned to make a dive to only 100 feet (30.4 meters) or so, until a buddy began pulling them to the surface. The narcosis and warm, clear water led them to continue swimming down with no regard for air supply or depth limits. There are also stories of underwater photographers so fixated by narcosis that they took dozens of photos of the same subject on deep air dives.

The only thing you can do about nitrogen narcosis is to prepare for it and account for it in your dive plan or selection of breathing gas. Setting strict limits on your dive plan helps prevent the temptation to go deeper. You should ascend if you start to feel the effects of the narcosis, although your buddy may notice the effects in your behavior long before you do and call the dive. The effects of nitrogen narcosis are comparable to alcohol intoxication. Every atmosphere of pressure is said to equate to the feeling of one dry martini.

The best defense against nitrogen narcosis is to either set rigid depth limits on your dive plans and not exceed those depths or to dive with a breathing gas mixture with a less narcotic blend of oxygen, nitrogen, and helium (tri-mix). Using this alternative breathing gas mixture requires training as a technical diver. Any time you breathe a gas mixture containing nitrogen, nitrogen narcosis is a potential problem. Susceptibility to nitrogen narcosis is similar to alcohol sensitivity. Some people feel the effects earlier and to a greater degree than others do. This doesn't mean, however, that people who can handle alcohol well are going to be less susceptible to nitrogen narcosis.

Vomiting

Obviously, one of the main reasons divers feel the need to vomit while diving is motion sickness or seasickness. There is no real cure for seasickness, but you can take a number of steps to lessen the effects of this sometimes debilitating condition.

Generally speaking, if you feel sick on a boat, you need to find a position that will lessen the influence of the boat's movement—usually the center of the boat, where the up and down movement is the least. You can also fix your eyes on the horizon, which gives your brain a reference to the movement. Do not try to read or look down while the boat is moving, or spend time below decks, where conditions can frequently be hot and cramped. Also, diesel fumes and other strong odors can make the feeling worse. Get as much fresh air as you can. It may help to keep something light in your stomach, such as a sport drink, juice, or crackers. Some people find eating or drinking products that contain ginger or peppermint, such as ginger ale or peppermint patties, settles their stomach.

Various over-the-counter and prescription medications can reduce the effects of nausea, but you should consult with your physician before using them and try them out on dry land before using them while diving. There is little research into the effectiveness of medications while diving, but the side effects (such as drowsiness, blurred vision, and dry mouth) may be worse under pressure.

If you feel nauseated before a dive, it may be better to wait until you are feeling better. As in other aspects of life, it's better to be safe than sorry. If you become nauseated during a dive and need to vomit , simply vomit through the regulator. After you regain control, remove the regulator and clean it out; then clear it and return to breathing normally. Many people prefer to vomit with their regulators out of their mouths. If you decide to attempt that, be careful because your first instinct may be to inhale—which can be a problem underwater with your regulator out of your mouth. Abort the dive if you continue to feel nauseated after vomiting.

Disorientation

In some diving situations it is easy to become disoriented, such as when crossing a sandy or muddy bottom with few reference features, or when silt or sand compromises visibility. Lack of visibility during a dive is similar to a whiteout during a snowstorm. Drivers often drive off a road in whiteout conditions because they can't tell which direction to turn; without proper visual orientation, divers tend to swim in circles.

FIGURE 4.3 Ripples in the sand, which form parallel to the shore, can help you regain your sense of direction.

If you are diving on a sandy bottom and are confused about which way to swim, look for sand ripples (see figure 4.3). They will generally run parallel to the beach. You can also feel for a surge as waves roll past, heading toward the beach. A compass is an obvious choice for reorienting yourself, but you must practice and become accomplished using it.

Other situations in which divers begin to feel disoriented are during a descent to the bottom on a deep dive, or during an ascent to the surface. Episodes of low visibility can leave divers unsure of which way is up. If you start to feel confused in the water, before you do anything, *stop, think, and breathe*. If possible, hold on to a fixed object and signal your buddy. Take a deep breath and relax. Remember that bubbles rise. If there is any water in your mask, it will act as a bubble level. Also, the weights in your belt pull down and your BCD pulls up. If you remember these facts, you will be able to get your bearings. Not having a bottom reference can be especially stressful for new or inexperienced divers, or for those returning to the water after a period of absence from the sport. Therefore, the first dive for such divers should be at a location where a bottom reference is available from the beginning of the dive.

Fatigue

If you find yourself getting fatigued during a dive because you've been working too hard because of buoyancy problems or currents underwater, the first thing you should do is take a deep breath and try to relax. Remember, the best way to deal with a stressful situation is to *stop, think,* and *breathe*—and *then act.* If possible, grab hold of a rock or the wreck to stabilize yourself and regain your composure.

Getting tired while diving can quickly lead to other problems such as hyperventilation if you don't get yourself or the situation under control. You should breathe normally and slowly and ascend with your buddy to the surface, fulfilling any decompression obligation. Once you reach the surface, make yourself positively buoyant by inflating your BCD or dropping your weights, if it is an emergency. If you are in danger, you should also jettison anything that could compromise your safety.

PART II

Rescue Techniques

5

Missing Diver Search

Divers can become separated from their buddies for a number of reasons, although in most cases it comes down to poor dive planning, inattentiveness, or buddies with incompatible goals. For example, pairing a diver who likes to swim fast and cover as much ground as possible with an underwater photographer is probably a recipe for problems. It is important to remember that you and your diving companion should be close enough during the dive so that either of you can reach the other if an event in which assistance is needed (such as an out-of-air emergency) should occur.

Most of the time when two divers become separated, they are apart for only brief periods and are still close enough to provide assistance if necessary. On dives with relatively clear water, divers sometimes feel that they are close enough if they can see each other. Should a catastrophic event such as an out-of-air emergency occur, however, the distance between two the divers may be a long way to swim.

If two divers become separated for more than a minute or two, then the situation becomes more serious. The missing diver may be lost or in trouble. Given the fact that you have a limited air supply, there is no time to waste when initiating a search.

Looking for a Lost Buddy

If you and your buddy become separated, immediately stop and turn in a complete circle, looking and listening for your buddy for approximately one minute. As you do so, you can initiate any attention-getting procedures you and your buddy agreed upon prior to the dive. This could include banging

Dive buddies should stay together so that they can respond easily to one another in an emergency.

on your tank with your knife or taking another action that will attract attention. If you can't find your buddy during this time, you should ascend slowly while rotating, looking for bubbles or other signs that your buddy is nearby. Continue until you reach the surface and then look for your buddy's bubbles on the surface.

Hopefully, your buddy will have realized that you are separated and will have begun following the same procedure, per your predive preparation. If this is the case, you should both surface about the same time. If your buddy doesn't show up, then where you ascended becomes the starting point for your search. Slowly turn around and look for your buddy's bubbles. It may be difficult to see them from the water. After a minute or two, if you can't detect any sign of your missing buddy, you should alert others on the shore or on the boat to begin a search. They may be able to spot your buddy's bubbles from their higher vantage point.

Leading a Search

If you are on the boat or on shore when a member of a buddy team alerts you that a diver has gone missing, you will need to take charge. Begin by getting the missing diver's partner out of the water and finding out when she last saw her buddy, what they were doing, and which direction they were headed. All of that information forms the basis of your search.

If a diver surfaces as soon as she realizes she has lost contact with her buddy, get a marker buoy in the water and use your compass to take a bearing on the diver's location relevant to objects that don't move, as shown in figure 5.1. It is best to take two bearings on different objects, if possible, to get a fix on the location. Assuming the diver ascended directly to the surface as soon as she realized her buddy was missing, that is your starting point.

Have spotters scan the surface and look for bubbles, if the lost diver was using standard open-circuit scuba equipment and not a closed-circuit rebreather, which would not exhaust bubbles. The spotters should climb as high up as they can, to the flying bridge or the upper deck. They should look in every possible direction, but they should especially pay attention to the horizon downcurrent from where the missing diver's buddy surfaced. If the spotters find bubbles, send a diver to check them out. They may be from other divers, but they could be from your missing diver.

Find out what was happening just before the buddy pair lost contact, how long they were separated, and where they were the last time the diver saw her buddy. You also need to find out whether the missing diver was acting unusually or if there was any indication that anything was wrong. If you are diving from the shore, someone should check to see whether the missing diver's equipment bag is still there and check on her car. Divers have been known to surface from a dive and leave the scene without telling anyone. If you are diving from a boat, check with other vessels in the vicinity to see if the missing diver mistakenly boarded the wrong boat.

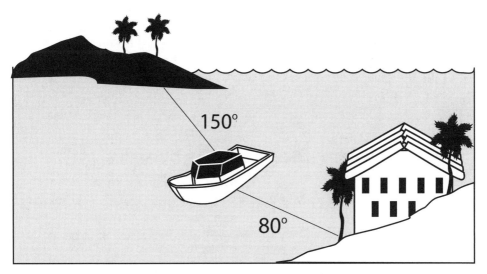

FIGURE 5.1 When conducting a missing diver search, establish bearings on immobile objects; doing so allows you or other searchers to return to or remain in the same spot during the course of the search.

You'll also want to get a description of the diver's equipment—BCD, tank and wetsuit colors, gear type and configuration—anything that will aid the searchers in identifying the missing diver. You don't want the searchers to confuse the missing diver with another searcher.

Underwater searchers should work in pairs. Doing so is safer for the searchers, and will avoid their confusing a solo searcher with the missing diver. Search divers must have adequate air supplies and bottom time to safely conduct a search. The last thing you need is for a diver to get in decompression trouble or run out of air while looking for a missing diver. Set an agreed-on time limit for the search before the divers get in the water. Estimate how long the missing diver's air could have lasted and, if their search plan permits, have the divers search for 30 minutes beyond that. If there's any possibility that the missing diver could have found an air source somewhere, you could search longer, but don't jeopardize the rescuers in the process.

It is also a good idea to keep a standby buddy team on the surface, if you have enough people. If the searchers locate the diver underwater, but can't bring him back to the surface, they can direct your standby team back to the diver. You should also have a diver recall system on board. The diver recall system can be used to get all divers back on board the boat or shore for a head count to make sure the missing diver has not somehow blended in with the searchers. Recalling all the other divers will also make it possible to conduct a search for evidence of the missing diver without having to rule out evidence emanating from search divers. Some possible recall signals include banging on the ladder or the inside of the boat hull in a prearranged sequence. You can also rev the boat engines or broadcast an alarm sound underwater using an underwater speaker. Brief search divers on diver recall procedures before they enter the water.

If your attempts to locate the missing diver prove fruitless, turn the search over to professional public safety dive teams. Recall your divers to the boat and allow the professionals to do their job. You should be prepared to give the public safety divers all the information you have on the missing diver, including the dive plan, time in the water, air capacity, and a description of the diver's equipment. All of this information will aid the dive teams in their search.

Using Search Patterns

If you decide that you can safely conduct your own search, you must act quickly. When setting up a search pattern, remember that the best one is usually the simplest. The faster you can set it up, the better the chances are that it will work.

Choose the search pattern that will work best for the environment you're in. If you're working with a mud bottom and low visibility, use a search pattern that allows you to stay in contact with your center point, such as a sweep pattern using an anchor as your center point. If you've got a lot of ground to cover and good visibility, use the U-pattern. Depending on the number of experienced searchers you have, you can opt for search patterns that put more searchers to work.

Regardless of the search pattern you use to find a missing diver, there are a number of things you should tell your search divers. Instruct them to maintain good buoyancy control while searching and hover off the bottom to keep from stirring up sediments, further reducing visibility and the possibility of a successful rescue or recovery. Additionally, give them any information you have about the missing diver's equipment so that they don't mistake other divers for the missing diver.

U-Pattern Search Only divers who are accomplished using a compass should attempt this search pattern. Working in pairs, one diver searches and watches ahead while the second diver navigates. The divers swim a distance forward, make a 90-degree turn either to the right or left, and swim 25 yards (23 meters) or a specified number of fin kicks. They then stop and make another 90-degree turn in the same direction as before and then swim back 180 degrees from the original heading. Depending on the visibility and the scope of the search area, each short leg of the pattern can be anywhere from 10 to 25 yards (9 to 23 meters). At the end of the first U pattern (see figure 5.2), the divers can begin another U and continue working across a broad area. Different buddy teams can move out in different directions, covering a large field.

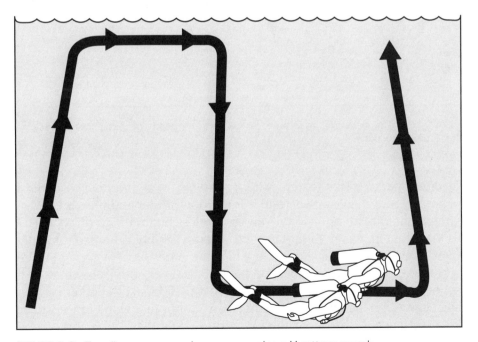

FIGURE 5.2   Two divers can cover large areas using a U-pattern search.

Expanding Square Working outward, with one diver navigating while the other keeps track of distance using kick cycles or breaths, the divers start from a fixed point and swim out one leg, usually 10 to 20 yards (9 to 18.3 meters) or a specified number of fin kicks. The divers then make a 90-degree turn and swim 10 to 20 yards (9 to 18.3 meters) farther than the first leg, depending on the visibility. At the end of that leg, the divers turn again in the same direction and swim another leg that is 10 to 20 yards (9 to 18.3 meters) longer than the last. The divers continue in an ever-expanding pattern (see figure 5.3). This pattern is effective if there is no current that would make an unconscious diver drift in any particular direction, and if there is a good starting point from which to begin the search.

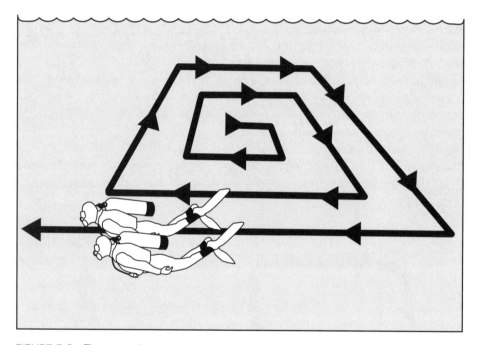

FIGURE 5.3 The expanding square search pattern is a good option for covering a large, flat, featureless bottom.

Circular Search This search pattern requires an anchor, which could be the anchor of the dive vessel, and a long rope or reel and line. It is a good search technique for a flat, relatively featureless bottom. Two divers can use this technique to cover a lot of ground where visibility is limited. One diver serves as the anchor for the circle while the other diver swims in a circle holding on to the rope or line (see figure 5.4). Every orbit, the diver at the anchor lets out more rope and the diver at the end makes another lap. Both divers can swim the circles if they have an anchor that won't move, such as the vessel anchor; they hold the extra rope while they swim and let some out with each orbit.

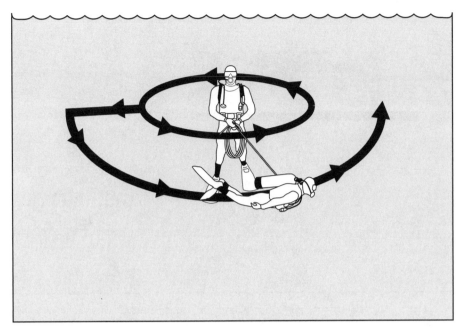

FIGURE 5.4 When visibility is low, and the bottom is relatively flat, a circular search pattern is a good option.

Random Search Because you have only a few minutes to put a search together, and because many of your divers may already be in the water, you may have to organize a random search. In some instances, a directed random search may be your best bet anyway. Often, your divers will be searching a confined space, such as a wreck, a coral outcropping, or a kelp bed, which would make it difficult to maintain a search pattern. If this is the case, simply saturate the area with buddy teams and see what they can find.

Remember that an incapacitated diver will not necessarily be found in an expected area. A diver who became unconscious on ascent, for example, may have drifted away from the dive site. You might find an incapacitated diver downcurrent.

Conducting a Surface-Led Search

A single person on the surface can control several teams of divers. Diver teams enter the water while the search coordinator remains on the surface, usually in a small boat (see figure 5.5). The search coordinator moves the boat slowly in the general direction of the search, maintaining a fix on surface locations. The search teams swim along the bottom contours, keeping an eye on the boat and maintaining a position relative to it (directly below it, to the right, to the left). Often, the divers in the water will swim forward, with lines attaching them to the boat so that the search coordinator can keep in touch with them.

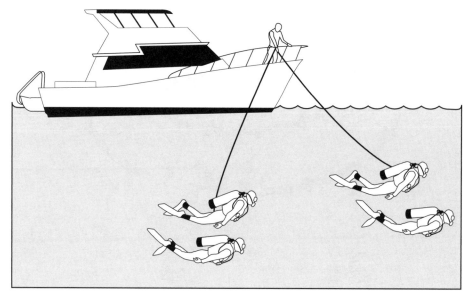

FIGURE 5.5 Multiple search teams can search for a missing diver when controlled by a coordinator on the surface.

The search coordinator can monitor the dive teams visually or by using the lines and can immediately notify the other teams via the diver recall system or the lines if one pair finds the missing diver. While underwater search activities are taking place, the surface teams should continuously monitor the surface.

6

Surface Rescue Techniques

The most important thing you can do in any emergency is to make sure you understand the situation before taking any action. There is nothing worse than reacting without thinking first. In other words, *Act, don't react.* Acting appropriately requires training and regular practice in the proper rescue techniques.

To properly identify a problem, you must first assess the situation. This, of course, doesn't mean that you need to consult a lot of other people and write up a detailed plan before helping out, but you do need to run through a mental checklist. Evaluate what is happening and why it is happening, what resources you have at your disposal, and what is the best way to deal with the situation. You must be able to do this in just a few quick moments, which you can do if you take part in regular practice, training, and continuing education.

With a surface emergency, you need to determine quickly whether the diver is conscious or unconscious. That may sound simplistic, but how you should respond depends on the level of consciousness of the diver. If the diver is conscious, determine whether he is rational and in trouble, or in trouble and panicking. Is he near panic? Is he struggling at all, or barely aware of the situation? In this section we will look at each possible situation in turn. Each one has its own complications and rescue techniques.

Rescuing a Conscious Diver

You're on the boat or on the beach, and you realize a diver is in trouble. Your first thought should be, "How can I help this diver without getting wet?" Dealing with another person who is in trouble from the water can be very dangerous.

Your last option should be to get in the water yourself. Your rescue steps should follow the tried and true: reach, throw, row, and go.

1. **Reach.** Find something long to extend out to the diver and pull her in. This can be a boat oar, a stick, a pike pole, a branch, or whatever you have handy.

2. **Throw.** Throw the diver an object that floats (preferably a life buoy, life ring, buoyant throw bag, or float) and is tied to a line. Get the diver to grab on to the line, and then tow her back to the boat and safety. Improvise if no formal rescue equipment is available. Any large floating items— fishing floats, coolers, (empty) sealed jugs—may help in an emergency.

3. **Row.** Use a small boat, surfboard, or other water craft to paddle out to the diver.

4. **Go.** Swimming to the diver should be your last option. Even if the diver in trouble isn't panicking, or at least not outwardly, there is a good chance she isn't far from it. The only rational thought in her mind is probably to find a way to remain on the surface. Without thinking, she might try to climb on top of you to keep herself from sinking. If someone must go out, and there are multiple potential rescuers present, the most capable and experienced should go while the others stay behind and assist.

Approaching the Diver

If you have determined that you need to swim out to help a diver, do everything in your power to enlist help before jumping in. Assign someone to serve as a spotter from the boat or shore, in case the diver sinks below the surface. Assign someone to alert the authorities, if the situation should turn serious, and to help you provide care when the diver is brought back to safety. You should also make sure you can maintain your own positive buoyancy. Carry a float, life jacket, or BCD with you or attach a rope or line to yourself. If you are in dive gear, don't discard it; it can help you if you need to submerge to get away from the panicking diver. Don't take the time, however, to fully gear up as long as you already have your BCD in place. Bring a snorkel and mask with you to allow you to breathe and see in the water should the diver begin splashing water in your direction.

As you approach the diver, swim with your head held high so you can keep an eye on him (see figure 6.1). This may help the diver relax too, as he realizes help is on the way. Do your best to determine the distance between you and the diver in case he sinks so you know where to search when you arrive on the spot.

On the way out, shout and offer encouragement. You may be able to provide some help while you swim by getting the diver's attention and instructing him to inflate his BCD or drop his weights. There are many cases of divers drowning where they were either unable or unwilling to jettison weights or heavy artifacts even though it would have saved their lives. Keep your snorkel or regulator ready to use as the situation dictates.

FIGURE 6.1 Approach a struggling diver with your head high, so he can see you and you can talk to him.

When you get close enough to see what is going on, you need to reassess the situation, try to determine the cause of the problem and get a feel for the diver's emotional status. Look for all possible causes of the problem, including entanglement, currents, rough seas, cold, nausea, decompression illness (DCI), an injury caused by a hazardous marine animal, and real or perceived problems with equipment or recovered artifacts.

◤ Orr's Safety Stop: Assess the Situation

If a conscious, injured diver is complaining of not being able to breathe, it may be due to equipment-related issues. Unzipping a wetsuit or loosening the straps or the cummerbund of the BCD may help. Many years ago, I was conducting a rescue class in the St. Clair River, near the town of St. Clair, Michigan. During the class, a diver (not part of my class) surfaced offshore and yelled for help. I swam to the diver's aid. When I reached him, I told him to drop his weight belt (which he did) and to lie on his back and relax because I was there to help. He tried, but complained of not being able to breathe. I decided to loosen his BCD straps and remove his BCD if necessary. As I did so, out from under his BCD came a rather large rock that he had put there early in the dive because he was slightly positively buoyant. During his ascent, the air in his BCD had expanded, pressing the rock against his chest so firmly and painfully that it made him think he was having a heart attack.

Encouraging a Calm Diver

Before you move in close to a conscious diver in distress, you want to confirm that she is calm. When you are within shouting distance, make eye contact and continuously talk to the diver. As much as you can, get her to help herself. Regardless of the cause of the emergency, be it nausea, a jellyfish sting, or exhaustion, her main problem on the surface is probably buoyancy. Divers often forget to make themselves positively buoyant on the surface when some other problem has them distracted, and then struggle to keep their heads above water.

Encourage the diver to inflate her BCD. If she can't do that, have her drop or release her weights or jettison anything that may be dragging her down, such as recovered artifacts or game bags. The struggling diver may be unwilling to jettison things she considers valuable, even at her own peril. You may have to convince her to give you a camera, game, or weights. Once the diver has handed these items over to you, you have a decision to make. If it is a choice between holding on to another diver's camera and safety, ditch the camera. After all, nothing is worth a diver's life.

As part of your assessment, attempt to determine the style of BCD the diver is wearing and whether it is completely inflated. Is she having trouble breathing? Remember that a fully inflated jacket-style BCD may constrict the chest, making it hard to breathe. Is she struggling to keep her face out of the water? A fully inflated back-inflation-style BCD can force a diver's face toward the water. If the diver isn't used to wearing a back-mounted buoyancy compensator or wings, she may not understand why she can't keep her face clear of the water.

Throughout the entire situation, reinforce the fact that you are there to help. Give the diver something to hold on to emotionally, without accepting all the responsibility. If the diver's buddy is there, enlist the buddy to help calm the troubled diver as much as possible while remaining at a safe distance.

After the situation is under control, you will need to determine what other steps need to be taken, including identifying the nearest exit point, determining whether the diver can get there unassisted or whether you must tow the diver, there and selecting a towing method. Those steps will be discussed in chapter 9, Towing and Removal From Water.

Responding to a Panicking Diver

Divers exhibit signs of panic for various reasons. The only thing you need to consider, however, is that the diver isn't thinking rationally. Panic has been defined as "unreasoning fear"; a panicked diver will use any means to save himself, including drowning you or anyone else within reach. The diver might be your best friend, but in a panicked state, the stricken diver will not hesitate to use you to keep himself on the surface.

Don't get too close if you have any doubt about your safety. Provide help with a float or a line and try to talk to the diver. Continually attempt to direct

◤ Orr's Safety Stop: Problem Solving

I was involved in a surface rescue situation in a quarry with extremely limited visibility. When I got close to the struggling diver, I noticed that his BCD appeared to be fully inflated. At a distance, I yelled to him that I was coming to help and that he should try to relax. Even with his BCD inflated, when he stopped struggling, he started slipping below the surface. I approached him from below the surface, located his weight belt (with some difficulty, I might add, because it was made of black wetsuit material, with a black buckle to match the rest of his black equipment), and pulled it away to jettison it. The loss of the weight belt and weights improved his buoyancy but did not solve the problem. The diver had a dark collection bag filled with very heavy artifacts clipped to the D ring on his BCD. It took another try to locate and finally jettison the bag of artifacts, which weighed as much as or more than the diver's weight belt. This is a clear demonstration that you may need to spend a little more time looking for anything that may impede your rescue attempts.

him to ditch his weights, inflate his BCD, and calm down. Let him know you are there to help. In this situation, you should consider approaching alone as a last alternative. If the diver is flailing around, he could easily injure you with his hands or knock away your mask, regulator, or snorkel. If the diver does succeed in grabbing you or climbing on to you, quickly submerge. The panicked diver will in all likelihood turn you loose if you go where he doesn't want to go—underwater.

As a rescuer, you should be prepared to step in without putting yourself at risk and help if the diver tires and momentarily stops struggling. If he suddenly calms down, he may be going unconscious and may sink below the water.

If the diver is conscious and actively moving around, but won't listen to you, attempt to approach from behind or underwater. You can try to swim around him, but more than likely, he will simply rotate and follow you. You will probably have to submerge and swim around to get behind or under him (see figure 6.2).

Once you make contact from behind, it is a relatively easy process to control the diver. While you are still underwater, take the opportunity to jettison the diver's weights and anything else that may be contributing to his predicament. To control the diver, lock your knees onto the diver's tank so that he can't spin out of your grasp. Inflate his BCD or drop his weights by reaching around in front. A fully panicked diver is unlikely to reach underwater to grab you. After all, that is the last place he wants to go.

FIGURE 6.2   It is often safer for a rescuer to approach a panicked diver from underwater.

Don't try to lift the diver out of the water using your BCD. Always inflate the diver's BCD first because you may need to drop back below the surface to get away or provide some other form of assistance. Once the panicked diver is buoyant, you can move away and assess your options. You have gained control of the situation, and now you can make decisions about your next course of action.

WEIGHTS AND PANIC

In 2003, DAN researchers, led by Dr. James Caruso, analyzed five years' worth of diving fatality data. Out of 285 fatality reports that included the status of the divers' weights, only 43 (15 percent) actually dropped their weights. The remaining 85 percent were found with their weights in place. Dr. Caruso stated in the conclusion of the report that "In the vast majority of fatal recreational diving accidents, the weight belt or integrated weights are still in place when the diver is removed from the water. Despite training to the contrary, the diver rarely ditches the weights" (Caruso, Uguccioni, Ellis, Dovenbarger, and Bennett, 2004). This study shows that panic causes divers to forget the most basic part of their training. Too often divers in trouble struggle to keep their heads above water, or finally wear themselves out and sink below the surface, when all they needed to do was drop their weights and relax on the surface, allowing the buoyancy of their wetsuits to support them. This information emphasizes the importance of regular practice of critical emergency skills, including jettisoning of weights.

Rescuing an Unconscious Diver

The steps for taking care of an unconscious diver on the surface are a little more straightforward than those for working with a conscious diver. However, that shouldn't make you any less wary or concerned about your safety. Your own safety should always be your first priority.

The odds of a diver becoming unconscious and remaining on the surface are fairly small. Usually, a diver who becomes unconscious will sink back underwater. However, if the diver realized she was going to go unconscious or might not make it to the surface and jettisoned her weights, she might float to the surface. Another possibility is that the diver was in a full panic and then exhausted herself. She might have passed out from struggling on the surface, only to float to the surface after she stopped struggling.

The step-by-step process for rescuing an unconscious diver at the surface is as follows:

1. Approach the diver. Always approach an unconscious diver on the surface cautiously (see figure 6.3). Unless you saw the diver become unconscious, you may not know what caused the emergency in the first place. Even if you did witness the diver losing consciousness, you may still not fully understand what occurred. You never know when there might be a dangerous situation below or around a diver that would put you or the diver's buddy at risk.

You will still want to shout and attempt to get the diver's attention, even though she appears unconscious. The diver may be watching fish below her and not paying attention to you, or she could be resting with her face in or out of the water. Shout at the diver, splash water, and make noise to arouse her or get her attention so that you avoid initiating a rescue on an apparently unconscious diver who is simply resting or quietly observing marine life.

FIGURE 6.3 Splash water or shout to see if a diver on the surface is conscious.

2. Assess responsiveness. As you reach the apparently unconscious diver, try again to get some kind of reaction. Shake the diver and call out to her. Try to arouse her. The diver may have fainted or lost consciousness, allowing her breathing and stress levels to return to normal despite her inability to respond.

3. Call for assistance. If the diver is unconscious, you should immediately signal for help. Regardless of whether the diver is breathing, you will need help. There is no need to do it all by yourself. Failure to use all available resources can put both you and the injured diver in jeopardy and reduce the likelihood of a successful outcome.

4. Establish and maintain buoyancy. Your next step is to make sure the diver is positively buoyant. This is best done with an unconscious diver by locating and dropping weight systems and removing or jettisoning anything else that is pulling the diver down (see figure 6.4). If you don't jettison the weights, you'll have to inflate the BCD to compensate for the weight, causing more drag during towing and reducing the likelihood of success.

Dropping weights can be difficult if you are unfamiliar with the diver's equipment. Weight systems integrated directly into BCDs have a wide variety of release designs that might be difficult to negotiate in an emergency. Independent weight harness systems that distribute the weight more evenly across the body may make it problematic for a rescuer to drop a significant amount of weight quickly. Weight belts made of neoprene wetsuit material may be hard to identify, as may be their release mechanisms. Therefore, as part of your predive preparation, you should learn how to locate and release your buddy's weights. Rescuers or dive leaders with a duty to care for others should quickly scan the divers at a dive site to see whether anyone is using an unusual equipment configuration, in case a problem should arise.

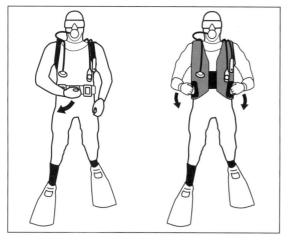

FIGURE 6.4 Panicked divers often forget to make themselves positively buoyant by releasing their weights on the surface. It may fall to the rescuer to release the weights of a panicked or unconscious diver.

Although dropping the unconscious diver's weights makes it easier to tow the diver through the water, you should not drop or discard your own equipment unless absolutely necessary. Dropping your own equipment may change your own buoyancy, making it difficult to perform a recovery if the unconscious diver sinks. Removing your own weights may cause a shift in your center of buoyancy, making your lower body buoyant and the rescue difficult at best. The same goes for your mask. You may need it if the diver sinks underwater, and it will make it easier to tow the diver through surf or waves.

A trained and practiced rescuer should not even attempt a rescue without the proper equipment. Before you ever get in the water to help, you should find whatever flotation devices and aids are at your disposal and use them.

5. Turn the diver faceup. While you are establishing buoyancy, make sure the diver is in a faceup position. There is nothing you can do for the diver with her face in the water.

If the diver is wearing a back-inflation-style BCD, you may have to deflate it somewhat to get her into a faceup position. Although that style of BCD is very popular in cave and technical diving and is excellent for keeping a horizontal trim while underwater, it may make it more difficult for the diver or the rescuer to establish and maintain a faceup orientation on the surface.

If you do have some reason to suspect a head or neck injury, you should attempt to keep the head and neck in a neutral position with the body while you roll the diver over. The easiest way to do so is by putting a hand underneath the neck while you reach across the diver and roll her toward you, as shown in figure 6.5. This process is made much easier with the help of a second rescuer.

FIGURE 6.5 When you encounter an unconscious diver on the surface, your first priority is to get her faceup and attempt to reestablish breathing.

It is highly unlikely that a diver would have a head or neck injury, however. Therefore, unless you have reason to believe otherwise, roll the diver over by pushing down on the arm closest to you while you pull across the diver's body from the other side.

Ultimately, neck injury or not, there is nothing you can do for an unconscious, injured diver facedown in the water. If you are alone, you should do your best, but you need to get the diver on her back so she can breathe or you can perform rescue breathing.

7

Underwater Rescue Techniques

Underwater emergencies bring an entirely new set of variables to the rescue situations discussed in chapter 6. The case of a panicked diver who is underwater is even more critical and dangerous than that of a panicked diver on the surface. The differences between dealing with an unconscious diver on the surface and underwater are significant. Generally speaking, you have less time to act and make a decision about what to do when an unconscious diver is underwater. Every second counts when a diver is unconscious, and probably not breathing, underwater, but there is little you can do for the diver until you reach the surface.

A situation involving a conscious and breathing diver in distress underwater is potentially the most dangerous for both the rescuer and the diver in distress. A panicked diver, who may have run out of air, will see you breathing from a regulator and will focus on getting to that air supply. He will probably not follow his training and secure your alternate air source, also known as an octopus. The regulator in your mouth is providing air and he may want it—and try to get it using any means necessary. This is yet another reason for regular practice of critical emergency skills involving air sharing. That said, the person coming to you, wanting your air, may be a stranger rather than your diving buddy, so you must be prepared for all possible scenarios including those in which a panicked diver makes a grab for your primary air supply.

Ultimately, rescuer safety is paramount in any rescue situation. We have said this several times already, and no doubt will say it several more. Take care of yourself first. Once you have encountered the diver and decided to help, you will have to gain control of the diver and get him moving toward the surface quickly and safely.

Rescuing a Conscious Diver

Whatever the cause of an underwater problem—whether a diver has a real or perceived problem; is lost; has lost a piece of equipment; is entangled in something such as fishing line, weeds, or kelp; or has run out of air—the diver could be stressed or driven to the verge of panic. This is not to say that any of these situations automatically precipitate panic, but anytime you attempt a potential rescue, you must be prepared to manage a panicking diver.

As in surface rescues, panic can be a life-threatening problem underwater. Ironically, divers are often found dead after a dive accident, floating on the bottom with all of their equipment in place and air still in their tanks. Every year case histories of fatalities include stories of divers who died in the sport they loved, for no apparent reason.

Problems that gradually escalate into a cascade of problems that lead to panic usually aren't emergencies to begin with. Uncontrolled anxiety and stress can result in divers breathing so hard on their regulators that they feel as though they aren't getting enough air, or breathing so shallowly that they create an excess buildup of carbon dioxide (CO_2). The result is hyperventilation and possibly panic and an escape to the surface.

When you encounter a diver who appears to be panicking underwater, look him in the eye and signal to him to take it easy, slow down, or take a deep breath. The most important thing a panicked diver can do is breathe fully and normally. Just as mentioned previously, when under stress, *stop, think, breathe*; and *then act*. To help the diver calm down, have him grab on to something solid—other than you—such as an anchor line, a rock, or part of a wreck. Many times this will be all that is necessary to get him to relax.

Because panic can result in tunnel vision or perceptual narrowing, the diver may not notice anything around him, including your signals. In this case, try to get his attention, which may be difficult. Once you have his attention, help him initiate a self-rescue and controlled ascent. Cautious but firm physical contact can be immensely important to calm down a diver who is under stress.

If the diver is in midwater and not able to grab hold of something solid, you will need to stabilize his buoyancy any way you can. If he is too positive, vent air from his BCD or, better yet, signal for him to do it himself. If he is negative, you must get him to add air to his BCD or, if a more dangerous situation is imminent, get him to drop his weights, on his own or with your help. Dropping all of a diver's weights while underwater should be done only as a last resort because it will make the diver's ascent to the surface nearly uncontrollable. Should it become necessary for the diver to drop all his weights underwater, you can help slow the diver's ascent with your own BCD or by flaring your body.

Once the diver, with your direct or indirect assistance, has stabilized his buoyancy, stabilize or control your own. Getting the diver stabilized and under control may be all that is required to manage the situation. Once you have calmed the diver down, you can work to correct whatever other problem exists, whether that means disentangling him, getting him oriented to the anchor line to initiate a controlled ascent, or taking some other kind of action.

When the circumstances causing the stress are under control and a controlled ascent has been initiated, maintain eye and physical contact with the diver during the entire ascent. If the diver is ill or injured, or not strong or clearheaded enough to ascend unaided, be prepared to swim with him and help him to the surface. Stop the ascent only if the diver's breathing is interrupted by vomiting, coughing, or other problems. Resume your ascent as soon as the diver is breathing normally again. If the diver has suffered a physical injury, such as a bleeding wound, apply direct pressure to the wound as you ascend.

In a true out-of-air emergency, the diver may feel the need to make an immediate escape to the surface. Obviously, the best option for the diver in trouble would be to make a normal ascent to the surface or to use an alternate-air-source ascent along with his buddy. But as a rescuer, you may encounter a diver who has run out of air, and you must be prepared to handle the situation. The next section of this chapter outlines the ascent options for an out-of-air emergency.

Trying to physically restrain a diver from making an immediate escape can be extremely dangerous. However, if you can slow him down and get him to use the appropriate out-of-air procedures rather than escaping to the surface, you may save his life. If you do manage to stop a diver from escaping to the surface, remember to exhale continuously as you ascend and, if you are positively buoyant, to flare out your arms, legs, and fins to produce as much surface area (and consequently, drag) as possible.

If you get to an out-of-air diver before he initiates an escape to the surface, try to make eye contact and calm him down. Provide air from an additional second stage (octopus) or a truly independent air source such as a pony bottle or Spare Air. Keep in mind that the diver may see the regulator in your mouth as the only working air source and try to take it away from you. Therefore, you should be prepared to access either your own additional second stage or an alternate air source for yourself.

Making Out-of-Air Ascents

One of the first lessons divers learn is to avoid out-of-air emergencies in the first place. You should always remember to regularly and conscientiously monitor your air supply, and to have a true and redundant alternate air source that you have regularly practiced using. You should also stay close to your buddy, and choose a buddy whose skill and diving habits are compatible with your own. However, should you or your buddy, or another diver, run out of air while underwater, there are some basic techniques to remember and basic priorities to keep in mind for making a safe ascent to the surface.

Normal Ascent

When a diver realizes she is low on, or out of, air, she should signal her buddy using practiced and universally understood hand signals and initiate a controlled ascent to the surface, keeping her regulator in her mouth while air remains available, breathing as she ascends to protect herself from potential lung injury. If, for whatever reason, the diver cannot initiate a sharing air procedure and must ascend with little or no air remaining, she should periodically attempt to breathe as she ascends, because the pressure change near the surface might allow her to get a breath from the cylinder. Also, the act of breathing may help prevent air from becoming trapped in the lung during ascent. If the diver chooses not to initiate an out-of-air procedure, her buddy should remain close by and be in a position to help, if necessary.

Alternate Air Source Ascent

A diver who is out of air should immediately signal her buddy that she is out of air. She should then switch to her own separate, redundant air source, such as a pony bottle or Spare Air, if she has one. Her buddy can also offer an alternate, or secondary, air source, as shown in figure 7.1. That source

FIGURE 7.1 In an out-of-air situation, one diver can provide air to another via an alternate air source while the divers make their way to the surface.

could be an additional second stage (octopus regulator) if the buddy has air, or a completely separate secondary air source in the form of a pony bottle or Spare Air. Any time a diver is using an octopus regulator, it should be marked for easy identification. That way, if her buddy isn't paying attention when the diver in need signals that she needs it, she can secure the regulator without assistance or confusion. Traditionally, the octopus second stage is positioned in the triangle between the diver's chin and ribs. Buddies should practice locating and securing the octopus second stage as part of their regular predive procedures during each diving excursion.

In an effort to streamline their equipment, many divers are using integrated alternate air sources or breathable power inflation system. This places a modified second-stage regulator on a very short hose as part of the power inflator. If an assisting diver is using this equipment configuration, he will have to donate the working primary regulator in his mouth to the out-of-air diver and switch to his own backup. Because of the length of the hose on this type of alternate air source, there is no way to donate that regulator to another diver. Although there is nothing wrong with this technique, divers and their buddies need to know each other's equipment so that there isn't any confusion about which regulator to donate if a problem should arise.

Common wisdom dictates that a rescuer who relinquishes his primary air source puts himself at risk. For this reason, the best way to resolve an out-of-air emergency is through the use of a truly redundant secondary air source such as a pony bottle or Spare Air. Having both buddies carry a completely separate air source is preferable to having two divers rely on air from a single source (an option discussed in the next section). Under normal circumstances, if the buddy team is at a point in the dive in which one diver is out of air, the other diver will probably be low as well. Two divers who are in a stressful situation and are breathing from one cylinder that is low on air will quickly empty the cylinder. Carrying a separate air source eliminates, or at least reduces, the likelihood that a diver will have to rely on a buddy during an out-of-air emergency. It does not, however, eliminate the need to practice out-of-air emergency procedures frequently.

When sharing air during an emergency, the two divers should make solid contact, possibly grabbing each other's BCD straps, and begin to ascend. Both divers should make sure they are making progress toward the surface. It is not uncommon for two divers to be so focused on providing air that they actually stop kicking and sink to the bottom. Alternate secondary air sources should never be used to extend a dive. Once any out-of-air emergency situation begins, the out-of-air diver needs to abort the dive and ascend, with his buddy, without delay.

Buddy Breathing Ascent

Buddy breathing is a situation in which the donor diver lacks an additional second-stage or independent alternate air source, but has sufficient air in her cylinder to donate. The divers move close together and face each other. They

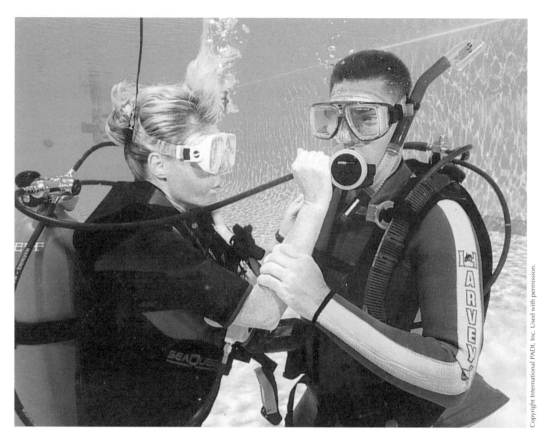

FIGURE 7.2 Buddy breathing is an option in which two divers breathe off of a single second-stage regulator. This technique is difficult to conduct and should not be attempted unless both divers have practiced it regularly.

take turns drawing two breaths from a single second-stage regulator while they both stay in contact with the regulator or hose (see figure 7.2). This maneuver is a complex psychomotor skill made difficult by the fact that some primary regulator hoses are not long enough to easily reach to another diver. Also, in an emergency situation, the diver who is out of air may be reluctant to return a working regulator to the donor. The result may be a double tragedy. If the buddy team has not practiced this technique regularly, and is not proficient at it, buddy breathing shouldn't be attempted. Keep in mind, however, that a desperate, out-of-air diver may leave you no alternative.

Controlled Emergency Swimming Ascent

A controlled emergency swimming ascent may be the best option when the out-of-air diver is relatively close to the surface and not close to his buddy. It can also be used when a buddy pair has become separated and one of the divers is out of air. Obviously, if a diver is close to his buddy underwater, the two should come together and secure the buddy's alternate air source, then initiate a controlled ascent. A controlled emergency swimming ascent differs from a normal ascent only in that the diver is unable to get a last breath from his regulator and is truly out of air. The diver should begin swimming toward the surface (see figure 7.3); he should not bolt to the surface or discard his regulator or other equipment. In this case, the diver should look toward the surface and make an "aahh" sound or hum while ascending to keep his airway open and avoid a lung expansion injury. The diver should also attempt to breathe through his regulator periodically, despite being out of air. As discussed previously, the change in pressure, especially as the diver nears the surface, may permit a breath or two, and the act of breathing may prevent air trapping, thus reducing the likelihood of lung injury.

FIGURE 7.3 A controlled emergency swimming ascent is an option when a diver is out of air and is not close enough to his buddy to get assistance.

Buoyant Emergency Ascent

When a diver in deep water finds herself too far from her buddy to obtain any help and out of air—two serious mistakes—and no other viable alternative exists, she may choose to attempt a buoyant emergency ascent. The diver should jettison her weights and begin swimming for the surface. The diver should look toward the surface and hum or make an "aahh" sound as she ascends to keep her airway open. As the buoyant diver nears the surface, the rate of ascent may accelerate dangerously. To slow the ascent, she can flare her arms and legs, presenting as much surface area to the water as possible (see figure 7.4) to increase drag. However, buoyant emergency ascents are truly intended to get a diver to the surface quickly and should get her there whether she remains conscious or not.

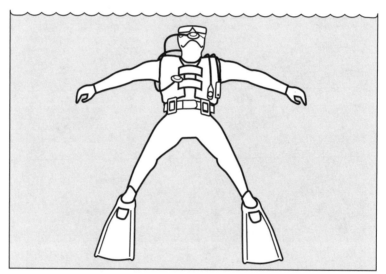

FIGURE 7.4   Flaring out on an ascent increases a diver's surface area and can slow an out-of-control ascent.

Rescuing an Unconscious Diver

When approaching another diver underwater who is motionless and appears not to be breathing, you should first determine whether the diver in question is actually unconscious. He may simply be resting, closely watching marine life, or preparing to take a photograph. On numerous occasions amateur photographers have been concentrating on something in the viewfinder only to be wrenched from their position by a diver thinking they had passed out. And sometimes equipment differences lead divers to mistakenly believe another diver needs help. Not seeing bubbles rising from the diver, for instance, could simply mean that the diver is wearing a closed-circuit rebreather system instead of open-circuit scuba.

CLOSED-CIRCUIT REBREATHERS (CCR): **A Special Consideration**

Closed-Circuit Rebreathers allow divers to breathe from a closed loop, removing exhaled carbon dioxide and adding in small amounts of oxygen to replace what has been metabolized by the body. While these devices come with their own set of conditions, they can adjust themselves to provide the ideal gas mixture for any depth, allowing divers to dive to deeper depths for longer periods while carrying small amounts of gas. Diving rebreathers provide their own buoyancy as the breathing gas circulates through the breathing loop and into the counterlung (see figure 7.5). To remove the mouthpiece from his mouth during a dive, a diver has to close off the mouthpiece so the circuit and counterlung don't fill with water, causing him to lose buoyancy. Similarly equipped dive buddies should understand this concern and know how to manage a diving emergency using this specialized technology. A diver not diving on a rebreather who encounters an unconscious rebreather diver underwater should also be aware of this special concern and be prepared to shut off the breathing circuit to keep the diver from becoming negatively buoyant.

FIGURE 7.5   Divers using closed-circuit rebreathers.

Just as with open-circuit scuba, if the rebreather diver's mouthpiece is still in his mouth, the rescuer should hold it there and begin the ascent. If it has fallen out, the rescuer should not waste time trying to reinsert it. He should, however, take a moment to find the diver safety valve (DSV) to manually close the circuit (see figure 7.6). If the circuit remains open, and the mouthpiece is out of the diver's mouth, it could fill with water, causing the diver to lose buoyancy and making it more difficult to get him to the surface. If the mouthpiece is out of the diver's mouth, the circuit may have already filled with water. Having difficulty getting the diver off the bottom may indicate that he is negatively buoyant. The rescuer may need to jettison the diver's equipment and weights to get him moving upward.

FIGURE 7.6   The diver safety valve.

Clues to a diver being unconscious underwater include the diver lying in an odd or otherwise apparently uncomfortable position. His arms and legs might be at odd angles, or his face, rather than being very close to the sand, might actually be in it. Obviously, if his eyes are closed, or open but apparently staring at nothing, the diver may be in trouble. If you don't see bubbles being exhausted, and you are sure the diver isn't using a closed-circuit rebreather system, you can assume he is not breathing and may be unconscious. Nevertheless, you should still attempt to quickly arouse the diver before initiating rescue steps.

Once you've approached the diver and determined that she is unconscious; based on your observation of equipment, lack of breathing, or an uncomfortable body position in the water; your next step should be to further assess his responsiveness. Touch the diver's shoulder or tap on his arm to see if he reacts (see figure 7.7). If there is no reaction, or a feeble one, your first priority is to get the diver to the surface. There is no real, functional aid you can provide underwater; the surface is the best place for an injured diver.

Never jeopardize your own safety when surfacing with an injured diver. If you still have a significant decompression obligation, don't make a rapid ascent, sacrificing your own safety to reach the surface a few seconds earlier. Even when bringing a nonbreathing diver to the surface, you should still make your normal ascent. If you need to make a safety stop or a decompression stop, do so. A decision to bring an unconscious diver to the surface without taking care of yourself could result in a double injury situation, or worse. Any injury to you during the ascent could seriously compromise your safety and your ability to render further aid on the surface.

Your complete knowledge of the overall situation, including your understanding of the capabilities of surface personnel, will help you make decisions that are most appropriate for the circumstances. If the crew on the surface is

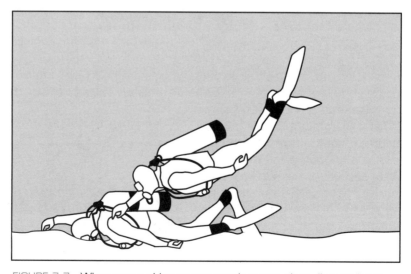

FIGURE 7.7 When approaching an apparently unconscious diver underwater, touch the diver's shoulder or arm to assess responsiveness.

prepared and ready to respond to an emergency in the water without your needing to alert them, you may decide to escort the diver as close to the surface as you safely can and then make him buoyant and send him the rest of the way on his own, while you complete any obligatory decompression. Obviously, there is a significant amount of risk to the unconscious diver in doing this as it presumes that surface personnel are standing by and will immediately take over. This option should only be implemented if missing obligatory decompression stops would put you at significant risk. This is a choice you would have to make in this type of life-or-death rescue scenario.

To surface with an unconscious diver who is not wearing a CCR, approach the diver from behind and get a firm grip on the diver's arm or BCD (see figure 7.8). You can also grab the cylinder valve or a handle on the back of the diver's BCD.

FIGURE 7.8 Your first priority in an underwater rescue is to safely bring the unconscious diver to the surface, but you should also take care to protect your own safety.

If the diver's regulator is in his mouth, you can hold it there, but it probably isn't absolutely necessary. If it has fallen out, don't worry about it and don't waste time trying to replace it. Get the diver to the surface without delay.

As you swim up, control your buoyancy so that you are not more buoyant than the unconscious diver, unless there is absolutely no alternative. Do not try to lift the unconscious diver off the bottom using your own buoyancy compensator or drysuit as a sort of lift bag; if you should lose your grip on the diver, you could ascend toward the surface in an out-of-control manner and be injured in the process. If the unconscious diver becomes semiconscious while ascending, be prepared for the possibility of panic and an ensuing struggle. Although the diver's regaining any degree of consciousness is highly unlikely, it is possible, so be aware of what is happening while you are making your rescue.

Some concern has been expressed regarding the potential for laryngospasm in unconscious divers underwater and the potential for lung injury to the injured diver during ascent. As a result, some authorities have recommended a variety of maneuvers, such as tilting the unconscious diver's head back and even periodic squeezing of the diver's chest during ascent. While it is true that laryngospasm could precipitate lung injury during ascent, the condition would be almost impossible to detect in an unconscious diver. Moreover, according to Dr. Richard Moon, Medical Director of the Center for Hyperbaric Medicine & Environmental Physiology at Duke and Senior Medical Consultant to DAN, the likelihood of lung injury during ascent is much less than that associated with the prolonged hypoxia the diver experiences as a result of the rescuer's attempts at these additional and time-delaying maneuvers (personal communication, January 2006). Therefore, our advice is to bring the unconscious diver to the surface without delay.

Once on the surface, make the diver positively buoyant, turn him faceup so that you can initiate further care, and then signal the shore or boat for help. Move the diver into a faceup, horizontal position in the water and then open his airway. Once the airway is open, check to see if the diver is breathing on his own. Occasionally, nonbreathing divers begin spontaneously breathing once the pressure of the water is relieved. If the diver does begin breathing spontaneously, be prepared to maintain an open airway. If the diver isn't breathing, you will need to begin executing surface respirations, towing him to care, or both. We explain both procedures in chapters 8 and 9.

8

Open-Water Resuscitation

Whether you come across an unconscious diver at the surface or you've ascended with an unconscious diver, after achieving positive buoyancy and orienting the injured diver in a faceup position on the surface, you have to decide whether to provide rescue breaths. Some rescue experts and training agencies recommend dispensing with in-water rescue breathing, preferring that the rescuer move the injured diver to the beach or boat as quickly as possible. That technique affords the rescuer a stable platform on which to provide whatever care is necessary, which is especially important when the injured diver is in cardiac arrest.

Open-water resuscitation is included as a part of the rescue process not because you should always deliver breaths during a rescue, but because it may be appropriate or necessary in some emergency situations. You will have to determine what you think is appropriate based on the situation, your level of training, your proximity to the shore or boat, and your comfort level in performing the actions. If you can reach additional help quickly, you may want to begin towing. Keep in mind that although the shore or boat may appear to be a short distance away, it may take a considerable amount of time to get there if you have to swim against currents, waves, or surface winds. If it will take more than a few minutes to get to help or a stable platform, you may want to begin delivering breaths on the way. Whatever your decision, the rescue skills you will need to apply require proper training as well as frequent practice and reinforcement. You and your diving companions should take every opportunity to hone these and other critical emergency skills.

Checking for Breathing

Once you have the diver on her back, you should move into the rescuer position (see figure 8.1). To do this, move close to the diver, preferably on her left side so that you can control the power inflator on the BCD easily. However, either side will work. Slide the upper part of whichever of your arms is farthest from the diver's head between her arm and her chest. Lock your upper arm between the diver's upper arm and body. This is sometimes referred to as the do-si-do position, because the way your arm and the other diver's arm lock together resembles the square dance step of the same name. Place the hand on the arm locked in with the diver's arm underneath the diver's neck. Support her head and begin opening her airway.

At this point you will have to decide if the unconscious diver's equipment presents a serious impediment to effective rescue efforts. If it does, you may wish to remove the unconscious diver's BCD or cylinder before initiating ventilations. You may be able to do this without compromising necessary buoyancy if the unconscious diver is wearing a buoyant exposure suit.

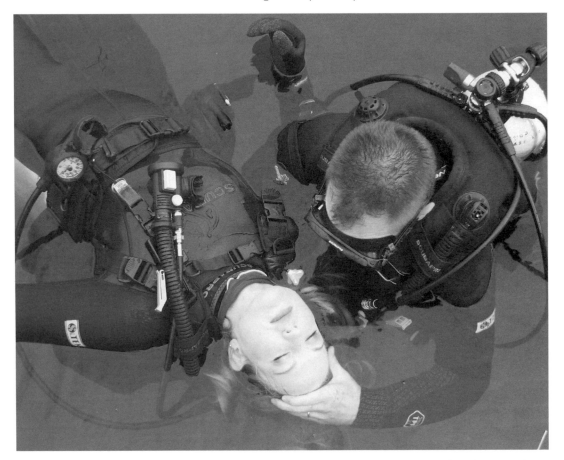

FIGURE 8.1   Use the rescuer, or do-si-do, position to move close to the diver, support her airway, and provide in-water resuscitation if necessary.

Your next step is to assess whether the diver is breathing. Even if you determined that the diver wasn't breathing while underwater, you should check again. With your other hand, remove the diver's mask and regulator. Sometimes, the simple act of removing the diver's mask, loosening the BCD chest strap or cummerbund, or reaching the surface and its decreased surrounding pressure can cause the diver to begin breathing spontaneously. If possible and practical, slide the injured diver's mask over your arm. You might want it later if the diver begins breathing on her own. If this happens, you can hold the mask in place while you are towing the diver to protect her from waves that might splash over her face.

Once the unconscious diver's mask is off and out of the way, place the heel of your right hand on the diver's forehead and move her head backward, opening her mouth and airway (see figure 8.2). Move your ear as close to the diver's mouth as you can and look down across her chest. If you are wearing a hood, you may need to pull your hood back or feel for the breath on your cheek while you look for movement in the diver's chest and upper torso. Check for the diver's breath for about 10 seconds. If you don't see, hear, or feel the diver breathing, begin giving rescue breaths.

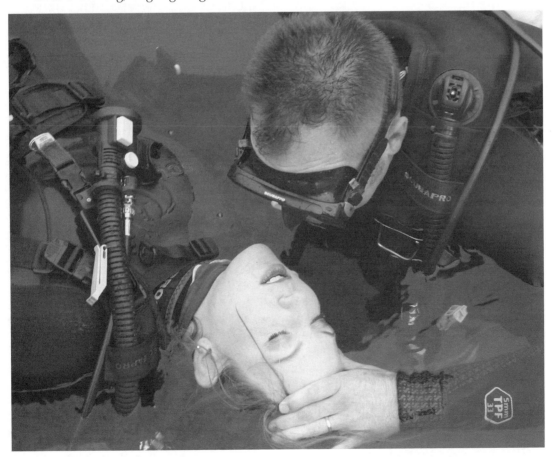

FIGURE 8.2 Use one hand to lift the diver's neck from below, and use the other to tilt the head back and open the airway.

Beginning Resuscitation

You can provide open-water rescue breathing in two ways: mouth-to-mouth or mouth-to-mask. *Mouth-to-mask* refers to rescue breathing using a resuscitation mask or similar barrier device. In today's society, with the increased concern about the transmission of various diseases, giving rescue breaths with some sort of barrier device is highly recommended. Obviously, mouth-to-mouth rescue breathing carries the risk of contact with another diver's bodily fluids, not to mention having to deal with vomitus, which occurs regularly in a diving or submersion incident scenario. Mouth-to-mask rescue breathing may also make it easier to get a good seal and control a diver's airway, especially in open water. The choice of which type of rescue breathing to attempt should be made before you even get in the water. If you plan to use a mask, you will need to make sure you have one with you and that it is prepared for use.

Having a barrier device such as a resuscitation mask available in a diving rescue scenario may not always be an option, however. Even if you keep one in your BCD pocket, it has to be accessible; and unless you've been meticulous about caring for the mask, it may not be usable when the time comes. One problem with keeping a resuscitation mask in your BCD pocket is the fact that it has a positively buoyant, inflated cuff. Divers have been known to reach into their pockets and find that their masks have floated away.

To perform either version of open-water rescue breathing, you need thorough training and frequent practice. In general, the techniques for delivering rescue breaths are the same for both, so we will describe mouth-to-mask rescue breathing. Where appropriate, we will highlight the differences between the two techniques. To begin, with your thumb and forefingers in the shape of a C, seal the resuscitation mask to the diver's face, covering her mouth and nose (see figure 8.3). You will need to press down firmly to completely seal the resuscitation mask to the diver's face.

When you have the resuscitation mask sealed, give two normal rescue breaths, each about one second in duration. Let the first breath completely escape from the diver's lungs before delivering the second breath. Leave your dive mask in place unless you can't get a good seal or deliver effective breaths with your mask on. It will protect your eyes and nose from water and spray. If you have corrective lenses built into your mask, you will need your mask to see properly. It's always a good idea to keep your own mask with you during a rescue. There have been many cases where rescuers jettisoned their own masks during a rescue attempt only to be compromised later when the injured diver slipped out of their grasp and was lost, or when they entered the surf zone and had to try to manage a diver with water in their faces.

In the case of mouth-to-mouth breathing, position your mouth over the top of the diver's mouth, while pinching the diver's nose closed with your right hand. If the diver is much smaller than you are, it might be easier to cover the diver's mouth and nose with your mouth. If you meet resistance when you attempt to deliver the breaths, reposition the head and airway and try again.

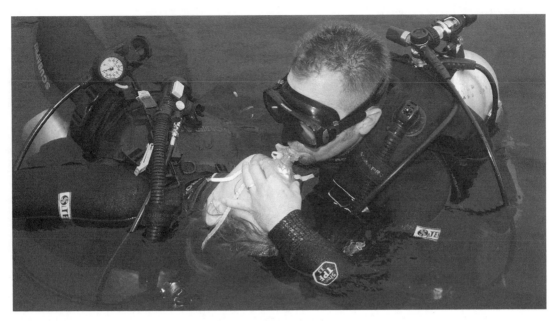

FIGURE 8.3 Press your resuscitation mask into position to create a seal and ensure that your rescue breaths enter the diver's airway.

You may not have gotten the airway open all the way the first time. If you still can't get your breaths in, check the airway for any blockage, such as vomitus or objects such as regulator mouthpiece bite tabs, then clear the mouth and try again.

If the diver doesn't cough and begin breathing again after your two initial breaths, continue to deliver one breath every five seconds. Fill the diver's lungs with each breath. Between breaths, maintain a positive seal on the diver's face and continually reassess for signs of choking and vomiting. As the rescue progresses, check to see if the diver's equipment is impeding your ability to perform rescue breathing. If the BCD appears tight, you may need to release the BCD chest strap or loosen the cummerbund to allow the chest to fully

MOUTH-TO-SNORKEL RESCUE BREATHING

Mouth-to-snorkel rescue breathing was heavily promoted many years ago, but was ultimately found not to be practical or effective because of equipment and practice issues. Most divers today use snorkels that allow water to drain out through one-way valves near the bottom of the snorkel. Delivering rescue breaths through these snorkels is nearly impossible. Many snorkels also have covers at the top to reduce the entry of water, making their use equally difficult. Mouth-to-snorkel breathing requires a lot of practice because you have to get a good seal around the end of the snorkel. Don't bother with mouth-to-snorkel breathing unless you are well practiced in the skill and an appropriate snorkel is available.

or adequately expand. However, be cautious about removing the BCD and scuba unit. If the diver isn't wearing a buoyant exposure suit, removal of her BCD may make it difficult to maintain surface orientation and provide appropriate emergency care; and if you lose contact with the diver, she may begin to sink. Don't overinflate either your BCD or the diver's. Too much air will make it more difficult to get close to the diver and to get a good mouth seal. If either BCD causes problems with ventilations, it can be partially deflated or, if necessary, removed.

In the water, there is no need to worry about checking the diver's pulse or signs of circulation. Your hands may be cold, the diver's skin may be cold, and wetsuits and drysuits make it very difficult to make a definite determination as to whether the diver's heart is beating. Also, practically speaking, there is nothing you can do about it until you reach a stable platform such as the boat or the shore. The best thing you can do for a diver in cardiac arrest is to get her out of the water and to a place where rescuers can perform CPR and defibrillate her heart using an automated external defibrillator (AED).

Towing and Delivering Breaths

While you are delivering breaths, you should begin towing the diver to safety and further help. There are two positions you can use to tow the injured diver through the water while delivering in-water rescue breaths: at the top of his head or at his side. In either position, kick down and back, toward the diver's feet as shown in figure 8.4. This will keep your head out of the water and keep you in a position to give breaths while moving you and the nonbreathing diver toward the shore.

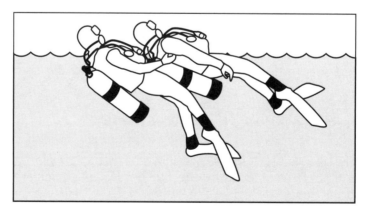

FIGURE 8.4 Use your dive fins to propel you and the injured diver through the water by kicking down and back, toward the diver's feet.

Head Tow Position In the head tow position (see figure 8.5), you cradle the diver's head in your lap while holding it with both hands. Positioned on your back, kick while you move the diver through the water and give breaths as you move.

FIGURE 8.5 The head tow position allows you to ensure a good mask seal and continue to pull the injured diver to safety.

Open the diver's airway by tilting his head back. Your hands will support the diver's head and neck. Hold the resuscitation mask in place using both thumbs and then ventilate the diver by pulling his head toward your mouth.

Do-Si-Do Position The do-si-do position is another desirable option when you are attempting to provide rescue breathing or when you are attempting to remove the diver's equipment while you are moving through the water (see figure 8.1 on page 92). You can add or vent air from the diver's BCD as appropriate to make it easier to give rescue breaths, and loosen or remove equipment if necessary.

Take your arm and cradle the diver's neck and head. You can effectively establish and control the diver's airway in this manner. Hold the diver's arm to your chest and swim on your side as you provide rescue breathing.

In either position, when you are giving the diver rescue breaths, try to establish and maintain a rhythm. If you feel dizzy, then slow your swimming or breathing and the rate at which you deliver your rescue breaths. The exertion of towing the diver and giving breaths may be too much. Don't exhaust yourself in your efforts to get the diver to the boat or shore. Signal for help at the earliest possible moment, and let help come to you, if necessary.

You may also have to adjust your respirations to match sea conditions. Rough water and waves may splash into the diver's mouth, further complicating resuscitation. Do your best, either with your mask or your own body, to shield the diver's face from waves and spray. Try to time your breaths to coincide with when a wave washes over the diver's face; you will protect the diver's airway by holding a seal and breathing for the diver while this happens. It is difficult to sustain rescue breathing while towing a diver for any length of time, especially in rough water.

If you have to remove equipment, don't be so focused on this task that you neglect your highest priority, to move the diver to safety while continuing to deliver breaths. You should remove equipment only between breaths. It may take several breaths to remove a small piece of equipment because you must first look for it, find it, and then unsnap it and remove it. Whatever you do, keep moving and get the diver to safety and additional help. Remember, you should remove your own equipment only if it impedes a rescue. Our experience indicates that, regardless of whether the rescuer is wearing a neoprene wetsuit or a drysuit, removal of the weight system results in significant lower body buoyancy, rendering the delivery of effective rescue breaths impossible. Also, if the injured diver were to sink underwater, you might not be able to recover him.

If a second rescuer is available, that person should take up a position at the diver's feet and push the diver while you deliver breaths. The rescuer at the diver's head is always in charge of the towing effort because that person will need to give breaths and keep pace; therefore, the rescuer at the diver's head should determine the speed of movement to assistance. A third rescuer should take up a position at the diver's other arm to help tow the diver through the water.

9

Towing and Removal From Water

Moving an injured diver through the water is one of the most important, but probably most overlooked, aspects of a dive rescue. Whether you brought the diver up from the bottom or calmed her down on the surface, the diver needs to get back to the shore or boat.

Towing the diver while delivering rescue breaths was addressed in chapter 8; this chapter addresses helping a diver who is breathing on her own move through the water. Which technique you use depends on several factors. Is the diver conscious or unconscious? Is the diver panicking or in a near panic? What are the water conditions? Is the water choppy, or are there large swells? Is there a strong surface current? How far do you have to go? Are you strong enough to move the diver?

After you have towed the injured diver to the shore or boat, your next step in the rescue will be to find a way to get the diver out of the water. This can be the most difficult and physically demanding part of a rescue—especially if you try to do it alone.

Out-of-Water Towing

It is always better not to get into the water to help another diver. Whenever possible, use a throw bag (also known as a rescue bag; see figure 9.1a), a tow line tied to a float, or a life ring thrown by a rescuer to pull the diver to the boat or shore (see figure 9.1b). These devices also allow dive team members on a boat to assist with in-water rescues.

FIGURE 9.1 When throwing a line to a diver in distress [a], aim just beyond the diver so that if you miss, you can pull the float back to the diver. To keep the diver upright and above water [b], use slow, continuous pressure on the line as you pull him in.

The advantage of using these devices are many, including less work for the rescuer and stricken diver, especially when currents or winds are an issue. These devices also give struggling divers something to hold on to and reduce the risk to a rescuer assisting the injured diver in the water. If there is strong current and wave action, both the injured diver and the rescuer may need to be pulled in.

One of the inherent problems with the throw bag is that the weight necessary for effectively throwing the bag comes from the rope in the bag itself. If you throw it and miss, you must quickly retrieve the rope, but because time is critical, you will probably not be able to take the time to stuff the rope back in the bag for another throw. A good technique is to retrieve the rope with both hands, piling it between your legs. If you have a bucket, pail, or basket, you can pile the rope in there. This way, it is in a compact form and ready to throw again. Some rescue instructors recommend looping the rope around your hand to keep it from getting tangled. As you practice and prepare to perform rescues, you will learn the technique that works best for you. Your technique choice may also vary with the circumstances of the rescue (time, distance, wind, equipment, and so on).

◣ Orr's Safety Stop: Throw Bags

The first time I saw a throw bag was during a whitewater rafting trip in West Virginia. Several of us met at the river outfitter's to get some preliminary instruction and were told, to our dismay, that the New River was at flood stage, but that we could raft down the more exciting Gauley River along with a group of guides on a training trip. My friend, an experienced whitewater rafter, told the outfitter that we were all experienced "water people" and would accept the challenge. Having never been on a whitewater raft before, nor heard of either river, the rest of us were at the mercy of our friend and the outfitter.

Our fate sealed, we made our way to the river and went through about 30 minutes of instruction and practice. We were told that a throw bag would be thrown at us if we were ejected or fell from the raft. If either event happened, we were to put our hand in front of our face to keep from being smacked in the face by the throw bag. As fate would have it, as we entered the first rapid, the raft was folded by a huge standing wave created by the flow of water over a large rock in the river, which had triggered a downstream hydraulic. I was ejected into the river and into the hydraulic itself. The force of the churning water kept me under for what seemed an eternity and then spat me out. I popped to the surface and looked around for the raft with both hands in the water. As I turned around, I was smacked square in the face by the throw bag, thrown by the guide, the only person remaining in the raft. For the next mile or so, the throw bag was used to retrieve the remaining five members of our band from the river. After that experience, I thought the concept of the throw bag was a great idea and started carrying a bag on all my dive excursions.

Shortly after this trip, I attended a rescue techniques seminar in which the instructor, Butch Hendricks of Lifeguard Systems, taught the technique of having the rescuer throw the bag beyond the diver in distress. This modification significantly increased the likelihood of the diver getting the rescue line and decreased the chance of the diver getting smacked in the face. I have taught the same technique ever since.

Because the bag has no inherent weight and you won't have time to stuff the rope back in, a good idea is to quickly fill the empty bag with water to replace the weight of the rope for another throw. You'll have to do this quickly because the water is likely to drain out if you delay. I know it sounds obvious, but make sure you or someone else has a secure hold on the end of the rescue rope so that you don't lose control of it while concentrating on getting one end to the diver in distress. During training people often watch the throw bag or life ring sail perfectly beyond their intended mark only to watch in horror as the end of the rope also sails into the water because they forgot to hold on to the end.

Although a throw bag is easier to throw than a life ring, a life ring provides buoyancy for the diver(s) in the water. In a pinch, you can use any float tied to a rope. Throw the float or life ring sideways with a forehand motion, or toss it underhand as if pitching a softball. You should aim for it to land just beyond the diver so that you can pull it back to the diver.

Your decision of which device to use will depend on what you have available and how far the injured diver is from the boat, dock, or shore. Typically, throw bags allow you to reach a greater distance, but they do not give the diver any additional buoyancy. The float or the life ring is harder to throw for any distance, but it gives the diver additional support.

Regardless of which device you use, pull the line slowly and continuously. Rescuers in the water should encourage the conscious diver to grab and hold on to the line firmly. If the diver is unconscious, the rescuer should grab the line with one hand and the diver with the other, and allow surface personnel to tow them both in. Throwing a life ring or throw bag may seem simple, but proper training and frequent practice is essential.

RESCUE THE RESCUER

Remember, during a surface rescue a lot is going on. Once an injured or distressed diver has been towed in, those on the boat should make sure someone looks after the rescuer in the water. This person is probably very tired or nearly exhausted, both physically and emotionally, from the rescue, especially if it involved a close friend. Those on the boat should not be so focused on the rescued diver that they lose the rescuer. There are cases where rescuers have succeeded in getting an injured diver to safety only to be lost themselves because they were too tired to help themselves out of the water and no one was watching them.

In-Water Towing

When you are helping a diver in the water, you may need to tow him to help on shore or on a boat. Don't attempt to tow or push the diver if he is panicky or struggling or if doing so otherwise puts you, the rescuer, at risk. In any of those situations, stay put and, if possible, let help come to you. The same advice holds if the diver is conscious and breathing, and help is on the way. If you are in a situation in which your safety or the safety of the other diver is in jeopardy, staying put may not be an option. (Techniques for dealing with dangerous currents are addressed in chapter 12.) If the diver is unconscious, you will need to tow or push him to safety, while protecting his airway from water, possibly by covering his nose and mouth as waves crash over you both.

To begin moving a diver, make sure he is positively buoyant and position him horizontally in the water if necessary. Inflate his BCD enough to keep his face out of the water, but make him comfortable. If he has air remaining in his tank, tell him to keep the regulator in his mouth to keep water out of his airway. Finally, use one of the following three towing techniques; the tank valve tow, the fin push, or the knee push. With a conscious diver, especially one who is uncomfortable, use a technique that allows you to maintain eye contact. This will help you keep the diver calm, or tell whether something is happening that requires your immediate attention.

Tank Valve Tow To perform a tank valve, or BCD, tow, both you and the diver should be positioned on your backs. Get behind the diver and grasp his tank valve or BCD once you ensure that the diver is buoyant by either inflating the BCD or jettisoning weights, if necessary. Kick toward the boat or shore. From this position, you can keep an eye on the diver, although it is difficult to see the diver's eyes. You should continually talk to the diver to keep him calm and reassured.

The tank valve tow (see figure 9.2) is probably the easiest way to assist another diver through the water, especially when the other diver is simply fatigued or exhausted and needs to regain his breath or strength to get back to the boat or shore. It is also a fast tow if you are moving through moderate chop because you are on your back kicking with your fins.

FIGURE 9.2 Use the tank valve tow to move a calm but exhausted diver to safety and aid.

The tank valve tow does have some limitations that can make it difficult to execute if the diver is panicking or upset: You are behind the diver and cannot make eye contact with him to calm him down. The diver may be unsettled by the fact that he can't see what's going on and can't tell where he is. Also, you can't easily observe the diver to see whether he becomes unconscious. On the other hand, this technique makes it easier to control a panicked diver in the water and is safer for the rescuer.

Fin Push   Figure 9.3 shows how to use the fin push to move a diver through the water. Position the injured diver on his back with his fins on your shoulders while you assume a horizontal swimming position. Place your face in the water and hold the diver's fins against your shoulders with your hands.

The fin push technique presents a few problems. Because of your body position, your kick may not be as efficient as the position described in the tank valve tow. You are also unable to talk to the diver while you move through the water. In addition, you must remember to keep your fingers out of slits or openings in the fins, because injury could result if the diver moves his fins quickly and your hands or fingers are caught up in them. Finally, this technique puts you, the rescuer, in a vulnerable position. Your head is between two heavy, large objects—the diver's fins. If he slips into panic, you could receive a nasty head blow before you can push him away. Also, there may be some difficulty keeping the diver's knees from bending, and all the diver would need to do in a panicked situation is to flex at the waist and knees and grab you. Therefore, an alternative method is to use your extended arms to push the fins, keeping them well away from your head.

FIGURE 9.3   The fin push allows you monitor an injured diver, but leaves you unable to continuously communicate with the diver.

The fin push is a good technique to use when you have two rescuers. One rescuer pushes from the fins while the other either stays by the diver's side and pushes at the injured diver's shoulder or tows from behind the injured diver's head. The rescuer near the diver's head should continually evaluate the injured diver and talk to him to keep him calm and reassured.

Knee Push The knee push is a modified version of the fin push. In this technique you, the rescuer, move closer, keep your head out of the water, and wrap your arms around the diver's knees, holding the diver's fins at your sides (see figure 9.4). This pushing technique is not as effective as the fin push, because you are in a slightly less desirable position to kick through the water and the bent legs create drag. However, you are in a better position to evaluate and talk to the diver as you move through the water. This technique also allows you some additional control of the injured diver should he become panicked, because you can control his movement by placing firm pressure on his knees. Keep in mind, however, that this technique has the same inherent risks for the rescuer as other positions that put the rescuer within reach of a panicky diver.

Regardless of the towing position you choose, if dive equipment impedes the rescue in any way, remove it. There is no particular method or order in which to remove a diver's equipment as you tow him through the water. Remove anything that hinders the rescue but doesn't sacrifice safety. You can release the cylinder to reduce drag, but remember that an empty aluminum cylinder is slightly buoyant so there is a trade-off. Also, the regulator is still attached to the BCD. In warm water, if the diver is wearing nothing more than a dive

FIGURE 9.4   The knee push allows you to control the injured diver as you move him through the water, but it brings you in very close contact, which can be a problem if the diver panics.

skin, it may be advisable to keep the diver in his BCD because the skin will not provide any additional buoyancy. With an integrated weight system, if you cannot jettison the weights alone, it may be best to remove the entire scuba unit including weights and cylinder. You will have to make a judgment on the spot based on the circumstances.

When you have decided to remove dive equipment, do so in a logical order. Don't get yourself in a situation in which you sacrifice effective swimming to remove equipment. Remember, keeping the diver breathing and getting him to help is the best care you can provide.

Generally, when you are simply assisting a tired diver, it is not necessary to ditch the diver's equipment unless it in some way impedes the rescue. Every dive rescue is unique, however, and circumstances such as surface conditions, towing distance, and your size relative to that of the injured diver will dictate whether to ditch the diver's equipment. If you are moving through heavy surf or kelp, you should seriously consider removing the diver's scuba unit. It creates a tremendous amount of drag and, if the regulator hoses are not controlled, can potentially get snagged.

TOWING WITH TWO RESCUERS: Three options

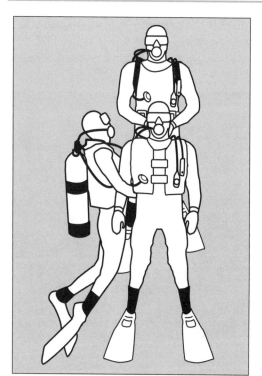

Two rescuers can work together to achieve a faster, more efficient tow. When there are two rescuers, they can position themselves on either side of the injured diver, one close to the diver's head in a do-si-do position and the other holding the diver with a forearm-to-forearm grip and in the swimming position (see figure 9.5).

Alternatively, the second rescuer can swim on his back, gripping the injured diver under the right arm.

In another variation, one or both rescuers position themselves in the swimming position, locked arm in arm with the injured diver, and push the diver through the water.

FIGURE 9.5 Divers using one form of two-rescuer towing.

Exits

As you are moving toward the beach, boat, or pier with an injured diver, you should do everything possible to attract attention and get help; shout, wave, splash water, light flares, blow your whistle or do something else to make noise—whatever it takes. You will need all the help you can get. If you are moving toward the shoreline, look for an exit point that would allow for easy removal from the water. If that's not possible or practical, make for the first landfall.

Although lifting another person even a short distance out of the water is difficult, it is extremely important that you do this as quickly and efficiently as possible, with as little strain on you and the injured diver as possible. If the diver is hypothermic or otherwise injured, you need to minimize the trauma to the diver's body. Additional trauma could cause further harm, sending the diver into shock.

If you have been providing rescue breaths for the injured diver (see chapter 8), you will need to reassess the diver quickly once you have her on a solid surface. You may need to begin CPR as well. You don't want to take too long moving her from the water to a place where you can provide further care.

Boat or Structure Exits

Moving a diver from the water into a small boat or onto a dock or pier is probably the most difficult exit because it will involve lifting the diver straight up out of the water. There is no best way to do it. You just have to use common sense and the tools that are available to make it happen with a minimum of disruption, disturbance, and potential harm to the injured diver and you. If you've been providing rescue breaths, the exit must be executed as quickly as possible.

Small Boat Exit With an Unconscious Diver
Lifting an unconscious diver into a boat by yourself is very difficult. Start by securing the diver's arms to the top of the boat, either by using a line or simply holding her hands in place, to keep her face out of the water. If you've not done so already, remove any of your own dive equipment that could make it difficult for you to get into the boat. Then climb into the boat.

Once you are in the boat and have removed any equipment that could impede getting the diver into the boat, lift her up by her arms, at the wrist or the armpits, to her waist (see figure 9.6). Once the diver reaches waist level, pull her forward, draping her across the inside of the boat and then finish by rolling her on board.

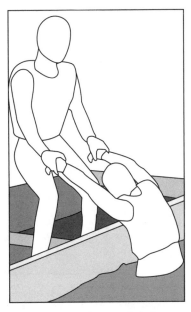

FIGURE 9.6 When assisting an unconscious diver into a small boat, enter the boat first and pull her in.

Small Boat Exit With a Conscious Diver If the diver is conscious and can climb into the boat on his own, you can hold onto the sides of the boat, duck your head underwater, and allow the diver to climb up your body and use your shoulders as a step (see figure 9.7). Alternatively, from inside the boat, you can drape your legs and fins into the water and allow the diver to climb up your body while you assist him. You should not attempt either version of this technique if the diver is in active panic.

Lifeguard Exit The lifeguard exit is intended for getting a diver onto a low dock or a swim step, or as the name implies, onto the side of a pool. To begin, place the diver's hands on the dock. Use one hand to hold the diver's hands in place while you climb out of the water and around him onto the side of the dock. Cross your arms and grab the diver by the wrists when you stand up. Uncross your arms as you lift the diver up and out of the water to the waist and drape him across the dock (see figure 9.8). Uncrossing your arms will roll the diver over so he ends up on his back. Then you can drag him the rest of the way out of the water. If you position yourself properly, you can use your leg to help ease the diver down onto the dock.

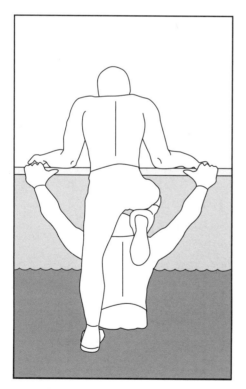

FIGURE 9.7 A conscious diver can use your body as a ladder as you help him into a small boat.

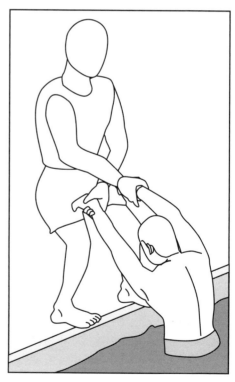

FIGURE 9.8 Crossing your arms as you pull a diver onto the side of a pool deck allows you to roll him over easily and begin providing aid once he is out of the water.

Ladder Exit If you are diving from a boat or pier that has a ladder you can use to climb out of the water, and the ladder is strong enough to support the weight of both you and the injured diver, you can use it to bring the diver up and out of the water alone. When using this method, remove any extraneous equipment from yourself and the injured diver that would add weight or make movement up the ladder difficult. The ladder technique is not recommended if the injured diver is much larger than you.

Position the diver so that she is facing you and straddling one of your thighs (see figure 9.9). Step up one rung at a time, bringing the other thigh up to the same rung as the first. The diver will literally be riding your first leg up the steps. This can also be done with the injured diver straddling both thighs with her arms draped over your shoulders as you climb, step by step.

FIGURE 9.9 If a ladder is available, you can use it to carry an injured diver up one step at a time.

Buddy Line Lift Another technique for lifting an injured diver onto a boat or low dock is the buddy line lift shown in figure 9.10. To perform this lift, wrap a short buddy line or a nylon strap behind the injured diver's neck, then forward over each shoulder, and then back under her arms. Bring both ends back up under the rope or strap behind the neck. Then grab the ends of the rope at a place that offers good leverage, possibly at the junction behind the injured diver's neck. You can bob the injured diver a couple of times to gain momentum and then lift up and back until the diver is on the boat deck or dock. This lift can also be used on precipitous shorelines.

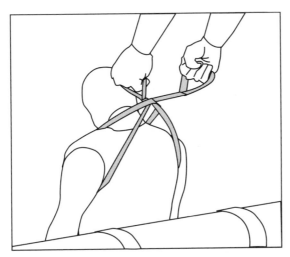

FIGURE 9.10 If you've got a buddy line or a short rope, you can use it to lift an unconscious diver from the water.

Roll-Up Technique This technique normally requires helpers and equipment, but it can be effective when you need to raise an injured diver a great distance to safety. To use this technique, you will need a tarp or a net and ropes. (One source of additional rope is the one in your throw bag.) With one end of the net or tarp secured along one edge of the pier, lower the other end, with ropes tied to it, down to the diver. Place the diver in the net or tarp parallel to the edge of the pier and then have additional rescuers pull on the ropes, rolling the injured diver up to the pier.

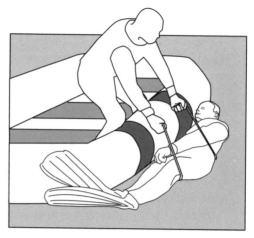

FIGURE 9.11 You can use ropes or nets to lift an unconscious diver up into a boat.

This technique can be implemented by a single rescuer (see figure 9.11) to lift an injured diver a short distance, such as over the gunwale of an inflatable boat or other small craft.

◼ Orr's Safety Stop: Drysuits

The advent of the drysuit created a new issue for traditional rescue procedures: If the diver experienced a suit failure, the drysuit could possibly contain water, adding significant weight and increasing the difficulty of the rescue exponentially. While practicing rescues for drysuited science divers during my tenure at Florida State, the rough edges of my hip weights once actually perforated my drysuit, completely flooding it. The rescue trainees moved me to the dock for extrication from the water. As they repeatedly attempted to remove me from the water, the gallons of water in my drysuit caused my legs to balloon out, making things more difficult and increasing my weight considerably. The rescuers contemplated turning me upside down to let the water drain out through the seals in the wrists or neck. I imagined what it would be like to be upside down with all that water draining out through the neck seal of my suit. I thought I might actually drown as a result of the rescue.

Luckily, they were able to get me into shallow water at a nearby shore position. As they simulated resuscitation, they opened the shoulder zipper and the water drained out of the suit. This is a classic example of the unique challenges that may require quick and creative thinking on the part of the rescuer.

Shore Exits

Shore exits are easier to perform than boat or structure exits because you are not required to lift the injured diver straight out of the water. However, you still have to move the diver across a wide beach. Consider the type of shoreline, as well as your size and srength in relation to that of the injured diver, in selecting the most appropriate carrying technique.

Surf Exits Making an exit through surf and breaking waves exposes you and the injured diver to possible serious injury. Timing your exit according to the approaching waves is your best plan. Large waves usually come in sets of three to six, about 10 to 15 seconds apart. After a set of larger waves passes, there will usually be a two- to three-minute period of smaller waves. Look for a place on the shoreline that will minimize risk to both the injured diver and yourself and will facilitate easy removal of the diver from the water. Avoid places with heavy surf or surge and places with a rocky bottom that will make footing treacherous. A gently sloping sand beach is best for these types of exits.

Plan to make your exit during the lull between waves. As you approach the surf zone, tow the diver from behind to watch the waves (use the tank valve or BCD tow described earlier in the chapter). If it looks as though a large wave will catch you, move seaward again and away from the danger zone. As a breaking wave approaches, turn your face and the diver's face toward the shore and hold on tight. If possible, cover the diver's mouth and nose and let the wave wash over both of you. If you have retained your equipment and that of the diver, try to make sure your masks and regulators are in place before entering the surf zone.

When you are making your exit, survey the area as carefully as possible to avoid rip currents. If help is available, position one rescuer on each side of the diver. You should never attempt to tow a panicky diver through the surf. Wait outside the surf zone until the diver calms down or additional help arrives.

When you have reached the sand and the water is too shallow to swim in, determine the best options for carrying the diver the rest of the way and onto dry ground to perform care. It may be as simple as dragging the injured diver onto the beach or shore. However, you may need to use an alternative method. It is best to remove as much of the diver's equipment before attempting any of the following methods.

- **Saddleback carry.** To perform this carry, kneel on one knee on the beach. Lift the diver up and stretch her horizontally across your back (see figure 9.12), wrapping one arm

FIGURE 9.12 Use the saddleback carry to move an injured diver across the beach.

around the diver's neck while you hold her legs with the other in an underhand position. This technique is hard to manage if you and the diver are similar in size or if she is bigger than you. It does, however, make it relatively easy to lower the diver to the ground.

• **Fireman's carry.** To perform this carry, crouch or kneel down while you are still in the water and swing the diver across your shoulders (see figure 9.13). Use the injured diver's inherent buoyancy to help get her in position. This carry is relatively easy to do, even when you are both about the same size, because your body provides solid leverage. Lowering the injured diver to the ground is difficult with this technique, however.

• **Backpack carry.** This technique allows you to essentially drag a diver up the beach by draping the diver's arms over your shoulders with the diver behind you as shown in figure 9.14. Squat down in front of the diver and bring both of her arms up and over your shoulders. Stand up into a crouching position and hold the diver's hands in front of you. Pull the diver's arms as you walk up the beach.

FIGURE 9.13 The fireman's carry is an efficient way to move an injured diver across flat terrain.

FIGURE 9.14 Drag a diver across a flat beach using the backpack carry.

Rocky Shore Exit If you find yourself in a position in which you absolutely must make an emergency exit with an injured diver across rocks or rocky terrain, tow the diver as close to the rocks as possible. Then turn the diver sideways, making him parallel to the rocks and as buoyant as possible. Watch the waves at they come up behind you and attempt to ride a swell up onto the rocks. Let the water lift you as you swim, pushing both of you forward. The wave may provide a slight cushion and let you down relatively easily as the water rebounds off the rocks (see figure 9.15).

As soon as you are over the top of the rocks, brace until the swell recedes, then roll or move onto higher ground, out of range of the next swell. You can then use a carrying technique, such as the fireman's carry, to move the diver to an area where you can provide care.

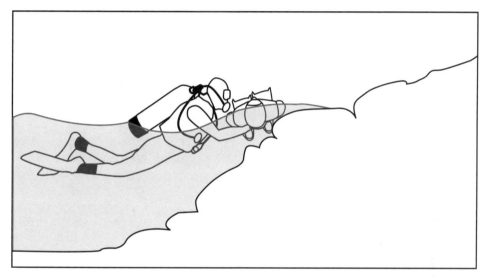

FIGURE 9.15 A rocky shore exit is inherently risky and should be attempted only when no alternative exists. To minimize the risk of injury, turn the diver sideways and use the wave action to lift and cushion both you and the injured diver.

10

Dry-Land Resuscitation

It should be obvious, but it is worth saying again that you can't do much other than provide rescue breaths for an injured diver until you get him out of the water. Chapter 9 addressed moving the diver to the boat or beach and then getting him on dry land. This chapter is a review of basic life-support (BLS) techniques—supporting the airway and breathing and performing CPR if necessary. It also includes information on the use of an automated external defibrillator (AED). Although our discussion here revolves around diving emergencies, remember that BLS skills can be put to use in many ways around a dive site.

To be fully prepared to come to the aid of an injured diver, possibly your buddy, you should continue expanding your diver education to include rescue techniques such as first aid and CPR. All diver training organizations and the Divers Alert Network (DAN) offer training programs that can be very useful. The DAN Diving Emergency Management Provider (DEMP) course, for example, encompasses dive-specific techniques including administering oxygen first aid, providing first aid for hazardous marine life injuries, using automated external defibrillators, and using advanced emergency oxygen techniques.

First aid, even first aid specific to dive emergencies, doesn't have to be complicated. If nothing else, simply remember to check the injured diver's airway and breathing and to take care of yourself. The rest will come as you get the situation under control. Keep a level head and allow your training and experience to guide you.

Basic Life Support

Providing care in an emergency can be exciting, demanding, and terrifying all at the same time. The likelihood of encountering a situation that would require you to provide CPR or defibrillate an injured diver is extremely small, but you should be prepared for that emergency just in case the situation ever arises. Your actions as a first aid provider can make the difference between life and death. If a diver's airway isn't open and he isn't breathing, then he will die. Taking some basic steps can reverse that situation and save the diver's life.

1. Assess Scene Safety

Your first step will be to assess the diver's condition. Your own safety is your most important consideration when providing care for an injured diver. Before responding to an emergency, quickly scan the area to see whether any hazards are present. Upon encountering the diver, assess the situation and ask some important questions: *Why is the diver unconscious? What caused the problem? What is going on?* If, after your quick assessment, you decide that it is safe to get involved, consider how to protect yourself. For example, take care when assisting a diver who has suffered a jellyfish sting; if tentacles are still present, they can sting you even when they are detached from the animal and out of the water. And anytime body fluids could be present, safety dictates that you put on gloves and retrieve a rescue mask in case you need to provide rescue breaths.

2. Assess Responsiveness

Once you are confident that the scene is safe for you to enter, you should assess the diver's responsiveness. Grab the diver's shoulder and shake him; tap him on the collarbone (see figure 10.1). Shout to see if you can wake him up.

If the diver is unresponsive, at the first available moment, put your emergency assistance plan (EAP; see chapter 3) into action. You will need to get emergency help as quickly as possible. If you are alone with the injured diver, call for help, even if it means delaying the beginning of first aid. It is extremely important, especially if the diver is in cardiac arrest, to get advanced life support on its way to you. Even if you have an AED with you, you will not be able to provide the additional support that paramedics, doctors, or other healthcare professionals can provide. Be sure to call for help before you start providing assistance, even if it takes an extra couple of minutes.

The only exception to the rule of calling for help first is when taking care of a child. With a child under eight years old, provide two minutes' worth of care before you break away to call. Children tend to suffer from respiratory arrest because of choking or some other airway blockage that can be corrected with basic life support techniques. With adults, respiratory and cardiac arrest may be brought on by cardiovascular disease, which will require advanced rescue

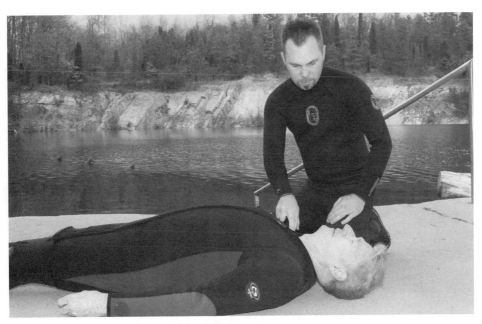

FIGURE 10.1   Your first step when providing first aid for an injured diver is to assess responsiveness. If the diver is not responsive, immediately put your emergency action plan into action.

techniques at the earliest possible moment. If the possibility exists that you may be called on to provide care for a child or an infant, you should pursue training specific to that age group.

3. Assess Breathing

Regardless of whatever else is going on with the diver, opening the airway and getting the diver breathing are your highest priorities.

After donning the proper barriers, open the diver's airway using the head tilt–chin lift method shown in figure 10.2. Position yourself at the side of the diver's head. Place one hand on the diver's forehead and grasp his chin with your other hand. In this position, rock the diver's head backward while you lift his chin upward. This opens the airway and pulls the diver's tongue away from the back of his throat, allowing the diver to breathe on his own, or your breaths to enter his body.

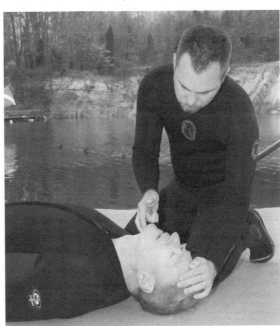

FIGURE 10.2   Begin the breathing assessment by opening the diver's airway. Use the head tilt–chin lift to bring the diver's tongue off the back of his throat.

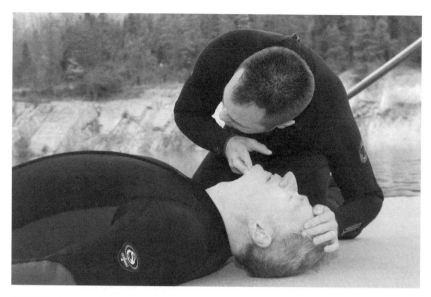

FIGURE 10.3 Take up to, but not more than, 10 seconds to look for signs that the diver is breathing.

Once you've opened the airway, you will need to look, listen, and feel for breathing (see figure 10.3). Lean over the diver, placing your ear as close to his mouth and nose as you can. In this position, look down across the diver's chest and look for signs that it is rising spontaneously. Listen for the sound of air moving in and out and feel for breath on your cheek. Do this for up to 10 seconds. If you can't see, hear, or feel breaths in those 10 seconds, your next step is to begin CPR by delivering two rescue breaths.

4. Deliver Two Breaths

To prepare to deliver rescue breaths, take your rescue mask or other barrier device and place it over the diver's mouth and nose. If you're not familiar with rescue masks, just remember that the pointed end of the mask should be around the diver's nose. Form the hand nearest the diver's forehead into the shape of a C. Use it to hold the diver's head backward and press the mask onto his face. Use your other hand to lift the diver's jaw up into the mask and press the mask to the diver's face. To use a mask effectively, you must ensure a good seal between the mask and the diver's face. Press down hard on all sides. If the mask leaks, the breaths will not enter the airway.

If you do not have a rescue mask or some other form of barrier device, you will need to decide whether you feel comfortable providing mouth-to-mouth breaths as part of CPR. If so, cover the diver's mouth with your mouth and pinch his nose shut to seal the airway. Obviously, mouth-to-mouth rescue breaths expose a rescuer to possible disease transmission.

Take a normal breath and seal your lips around the inlet on the mask, as shown in figure 10.4. Exhale into the mask with enough force to cause the

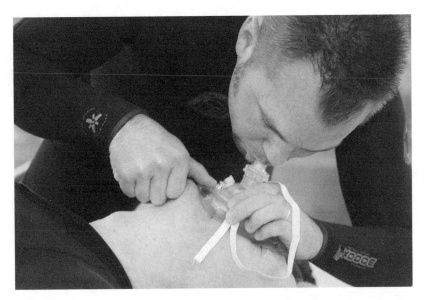

FIGURE 10.4 As soon as you determine a diver is not breathing, deliver two normal rescue breaths using a resuscitation mask or other barrier device.

diver's chest to rise. When you see it rise, let the breath go. When the diver's chest has returned to normal, deliver a second breath. If you have trouble getting the first breath in, reposition the head and try again. If you still can't get the breaths to go in, check the mouth for an obstruction. If nothing is obvious, go straight to chest compressions to see if you can dislodge the blockage.

5. Perform CPR

The current recommendation for basic life support delivered by lay providers is to proceed directly from the two initial rescue breaths to chest compressions. Essentially, as soon as you determine that a person is unresponsive and not breathing, you should assume that person is in cardiac arrest and begin CPR. Rescuers who have additional training as health care providers are taught additional steps beyond those that we address in this book.

To perform chest compressions, find your landmark on the body. This is the spot where you will press on the chest. Bare the diver's chest and position one hand in the center of the chest with your middle finger directly between the nipples. The heel of your hand should be on the breastbone in the middle of the chest. Interlace the fingers of your second hand with the fingers of the hand that is directly on the diver and then deliver chest compressions, moving your upper body from the hips (see figure 10.5). Do not attempt chest compressions from your elbows with arm strength alone. Deliver these compressions quickly, remembering to *push hard and push fast.* Allow the chest to completely recoil between compressions, but avoid having your hands leave the diver's chest.

Press at a rate to deliver 100 compressions in a one-minute period. This is between one and a half and two compressions each second. Perform 30

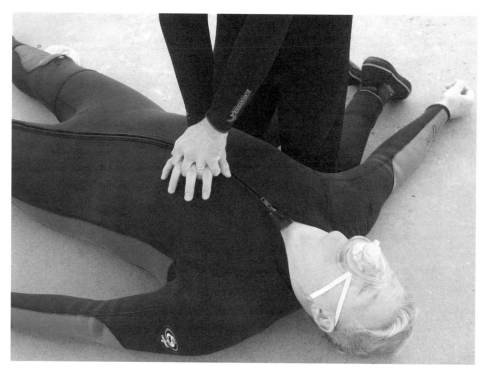

FIGURE 10.5 Using your body leverage to compress the chest, deliver 30 compressions at a rate of 100 per minute.

compressions and then pause to deliver two rescue breaths. Continue this cycle for as long as you can, stopping every few minutes to reassess the diver's condition. However, you should work to minimize interruptions, so that you don't stop needlessly.

Once you have begun CPR, there are only three reasons to quit:

- You are relieved by someone with greater medical experience.
- The diver shows signs of resuming spontaneous breathing or circulation.
- You are too exhausted to continue.

Continue giving the diver 30 chest compressions for every two breaths as long as you can. If a second rescuer is available, you can take turns providing single-rescuer CPR or work together to provide two-rescuer CPR if you are trained to do so. There is no difference between the one- and two-rescuer versions with regard to the frequency or number of compressions or breaths.

In the two-rescuer option, shown in figure 10.6, one rescuer provides breaths and the second handles the chest compressions. When the rescuer providing chest compressions grows tired, the two should switch positions and continue with as little interruption as possible. Although two-rescuer CPR isn't all that difficult, and in some ways it is easier than single-rescuer CPR, if you've never attempted it, it is probably best to perform single-rescuer CPR and switch off with another rescuer, assuming complete care for the injured diver by turns.

FIGURE 10.6 Whether they work together or take turns, two rescuers can more easily deliver quality chest compressions and rescue breathes without reaching exhaustion.

Automated External Defibrillators

In adults, one of the most common killers throughout the industrialized world is sudden cardiac arrest. There are many causes for sudden cardiac arrest, although the most common is heart disease.

When a person's heart enters sudden cardiac arrest, it commonly begins fibrillating, or quivering uncontrollably. This disorganized heart rhythm prevents the heart from effectively pumping blood to the rest of the body. The only way to return the heart to a normal rhythm is by using a defibrillator. A defibrillator sends an electric shock across the fibrillating heart, scrambling the irregular electric signal and allowing the body's own internal pacemaker to reassert a normal rhythm. For every minute defibrillation is delayed, the likelihood of saving a person in ventricular fibrillation, even with CPR, drops by 7 to 10 percent. After 10 minutes, the chance of a person recovering is extremely small.

Divers are no more likely to suffer from cardiac arrest than anyone else. However, because of the unique circumstances divers find themselves in, getting a diver to an AED within 10 minutes, is almost impossible unless the unit is onboard the dive boat itself or already at the dive site on the beach. Therefore, it is extremely important to have an AED readily available.

Because every AED unit is somewhat unique, it is essential to receive training in the use of the devices. Although they are made to be as user friendly as possible, for the sake of speed and accuracy you should learn how to use the AED that you will have access to. In the heat of the moment, you will want to be comfortable with the device. Attempting to save a victim of cardiac arrest can be intimidating enough without having to worry about whether you know how to use the AED.

After you have confirmed that the diver has no signs of circulation, you will need to bare his chest and dry it off if it is still wet. This may require cutting away a wetsuit or drysuit. Do not waste time pulling a wetsuit or drysuit off a diver.

Place the AED unit beside the diver's head on his left side. Turn the AED unit on and listen to its auditory prompts. Open up the AED pads and place them on the chest. Most AED units have diagrams right on the packaging showing you how and where to place the pads. Typically, one pad will go between the diver's breastbone and collarbone on his right side (see figure 10.7). The other pad should go on the diver's left side along the ribs at the nipple level. If the diver has a hairy chest, you may need to shave the area to make a positive connection with the pads.

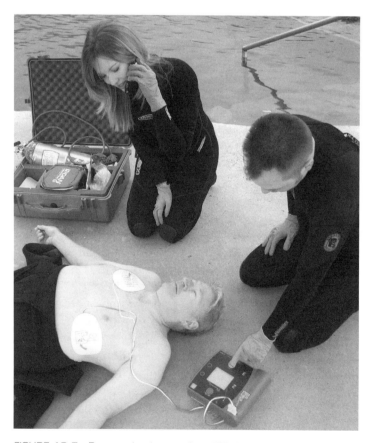

FIGURE 10.7 Proper, timely use of an AED following the onset of cardiac arrest can save a life. When a diver's heart is in ventricular fibrillation, his chance of survival drops 7 to 10 percent every minute.

Once you have applied the pads and plugged them into the AED, allow the AED to analyze the diver's heart rhythm. Follow the prompts provided by the unit. It may instruct you to deliver a shock. At that point you should both verbally and visually ensure that no one else is in contact with the diver. When the device tells you to do so, deliver the shock.

Current guidelines for AEDs and CPR from the American Heart Association (2005) indicate that even if the diver regains a normal heart rhythm after the first shock, rescuers should deliver two minutes of CPR (about five cycles). Even after the defibrillator has resolved the ventricular fibrillation, it takes a few minutes for the heart to regain a normal rhythm and create blood flow. A few minutes of CPR can effectively deliver oxygen and blood to the heart, as well as helping to build up blood pressure, ensuring that the heart will be able to begin pumping effectively.

Keep the AED pads attached to the diver's body in case the diver's heart should return to ventricular fibrillation, prompting a need for the AED unit to reanalyze the heart rhythm. Some older models of AEDs, built prior to the 2005 guidelines, instructed rescuers to deliver up to three shocks before resuming CPR. Do not attempt to override or outthink the AED you are using. Follow its instructions. The older guidelines are not wrong. Current science merely indicates that the newer guidelines are more effective.

If an AED tells you that no shock is advised, but you still can't find a pulse or other signs of circulation, you should immediately begin CPR. The heart simply is not in a rhythm shockable by the AED unit. AEDs can only shock a heart back to a normal rhythm when the heart is in ventricular fibrillation or ventricular tachycardia.

11

Diving First Aid

The ability to manage a diving emergency and provide care to an injured diver does not come from experience alone. The best thing you can do to prepare for dive-related injuries is to learn everything you can about such injuries and the situations that may lead to them.

Continue your education by taking advanced dive and rescue courses. You should also take specialized courses in the use of emergency oxygen, AED use, hazardous marine life injuries, and field neurological assessments. Local dive centers and instructors may offer these courses in your area. You can also contact DAN for qualified instructors in these programs.

Although you should be thoroughly prepared for any kind of emergency, case histories of diving accidents indicate that full-blown emergencies in which rescuers need to perform CPR and evacuate injured divers in a critical rush to a hospital are rare. Cuts, scrapes, overheating, and the need to provide emergency oxygen first aid are much more common. Of course, being prepared to deal with these more mundane situations will help you to feel more confident when faced with a serious emergency.

The skills outlined in this chapter are useful in many situations besides those that involve an injured diver. A bubble watcher may slip and fall while climbing over rocks to keep an eye on the divers and cut his leg, or a child playing in the sun may get too hot and begin to feel sick. This chapter addresses many of the common first aid problems and actions you can take in and around a dive site to care for divers and others.

Control of Bleeding

Divers can end up bleeding in the water for a number of reasons—from accidental encounters with sharp edges on shipwrecks or coral and rock reefs to encounters with dangerous marine life. Regardless of the cause, you should follow the same procedure for dealing with wounds and bleeding:

1. **Ensure an open airway and breathing.** A conscious, talking (maybe yelling) diver has an open airway and is breathing. If the diver is unconscious, you must first attend to the airway and breathing before you worry about bleeding. Although the bleeding may look dramatic, it will never be more life threatening than respiratory arrest.

2. **Protect yourself.** Use barrier devices (gloves and a mask) if there is a possibility of coming into contact with blood or other bodily fluids. If you don't have medical gloves, you can use your dive gloves to provide an additional barrier, although the thickness of the gloves may make care more difficult.

3. **Apply direct pressure to the wound.** You can apply direct pressure to the wound with a gloved hand or ask the diver to do it himself while you get your gloves on. As soon as possible, press a sterile, absorbent dressing against the wound to help control bleeding and aid the clotting process (see figure 11.1). If the first dressing becomes soaked with blood, leave it in place and apply a second one directly on top. Once the bleeding has stopped, use a pressure bandage to hold your dressings in place (see figure 11.2).

If it will be a long period (many hours or a day or more) before you reach professional medical care, you can remove the dressings and clean the wound. This will help reduce the risk of infection. However, if you will be delayed only a few hours, it is best to leave the dressings in place. Pulling a dressing off the wound can cause the wound to begin bleeding again.

Although it is best to use clean and sterile dressings to care for wounds, you can use whatever you have available. If you don't have gauze bandages, use a clean cloth or towel, or even a shirt. Straps, pieces of wetsuits, or other devices can be useful for holding the bandage in place once the bleeding has stopped. Do not, however, attempt to use a belt or a strap as a tourniquet. Tourniquets are problematic, potentially causing more harm than good. They should be used only by emergency care providers specifically trained in wilderness medicine. Also, except in extreme circumstances, they are unnecessary. Bleeding will normally stop with direct pressure.

Anytime you suffer a cut or laceration in the water, regardless of the source of the wound, immediately apply direct pressure underwater, attract your buddy's attention, and abort the dive. Make a normal ascent and get help immediately. Once the bleeding is controlled, clean the wound out with soap and water and bandage with a clean, dry dressing. Water is full of bacteria that may cause

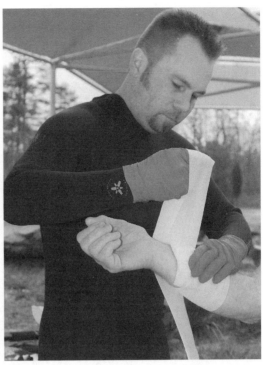

FIGURE 11.1   Control bleeding by applying a sterile dressing and direct pressure to the wound site to aid clotting.

FIGURE 11.2   Once the bleeding is under control, apply a pressure bandage to secure the dressings and keep the wound from reopening.

infections in an open wound. If you see signs of infection, such as fever, pus, or a foul odor, get the wound evaluated by a medical professional. Whenever you're in doubt, seek medical attention.

Shock Management

The condition known as shock can happen for many reasons and may be as dangerous to the diver as a physical injury. Regardless of the cause, shock is defined as an inadequate supply of blood in the body. When the body is dealing with a serious infection or an allergic reaction, it may dilate the blood vessels, leaving an inadequate volume of blood for the heart to circulate. This also happens with heat-related illnesses and, of course, bleeding. When the blood volume drops, the heart cannot pump effectively to circulate oxygenated blood throughout the body.

Whatever the cause of shock, your role as a first aid provider is relatively simple. You should monitor the diver's airway, breathing, and circulation. If possible, have the diver lie down and then elevate his feet about a foot to a foot and a half (30 to 45 centimeters; see figure 11.3). However, if this causes pain or breathing difficulty, lower his feet back down. Keep the diver warm

FIGURE 11.3 Handle shock by supporting the diver's airway, keeping him warm, and providing emergency oxygen.

and provide emergency oxygen. Beyond that, you should treat any other conditions that might cause shock. Never give an injured diver who is in shock anything to drink, because the person may not be fully in control of his airway and attempting to drink may cause him to choke.

Decompression Illness

Although cuts, sprains, and bruises are the most common injuries you will encounter at a dive site, decompression illness (DCI) is a serious condition that you must be prepared for. DCI encompasses both arterial gas embolism and decompression sickness.

Arterial gas embolism (AGE) is caused by overexpansion of the lungs, forcing air (or gas) into the arterial circulation. From there, the bubbles can enter cardiac circulation, causing symptoms that may resemble a heart attack, or into the cranial circulation, causing stroke-like symptoms. Generally, AGE occurs when air or breathing gas overexpands in a diver's lungs on ascent. Expanding gas damages lung tissue and enters the bloodstream directly. AGE can be caused by the diver holding his breath on ascent.

Decompression sickness (DCS), on the other hand, is caused by bubbles of nitrogen that form directly in the tissues or bloodstream as the diver ascends and the pressure surrounding the body is reduced. These bubbles cause blockages in circulation, producing symptoms ranging from skin rash and tingling to more severe stroke-like symptoms. Symptoms of DCS may be subtle and varied.

Although it might be important for physicians at a hyperbaric chamber to diagnose which specific form of DCI an injured diver is experiencing, from the perspective of the rescuer and first aid provider, there is no need to make a distinction. In the field, you will manage both conditions the same way.

Once your initial assessment is out of the way and you have confirmed that the diver is breathing (she'll probably be talking to you), you will want to look for a number of signs of DCI. Unfortunately, there is no single definitive sign that a diver is suffering from DCI. However, according to Divers Alert Network statistics, if a person has been diving within the last 24 hours and presents one or more of the following signs and symptoms, she may well be suffering from DCI:

- **Numbness and tingling.** This most often occurs in the extremities and may feel as though that part has fallen asleep or a funny bone has been hit.
- **Pain.** This can be a dull, sharp, boring, or aching sensation in or around a joint or muscle that does not generally change with movement. It can affect any joint or muscle, although shoulders and elbows tend to be common.
- **Postdive headaches.** These are common and typically ambiguous. They may be the result of exposure to the sun, a pressure-related injury of the sinus cavity, such as a sinus squeeze, carbon dioxide retention, or decompression illness. Headaches associated with DCI often are accompanied by other symptoms.
- **Dizziness and vertigo.** This refers to a feeling of spinning and can lead to a loss of balance.
- **Fatigue.** The fatigue that is associated with DCI is more severe than normal and out of proportion to the exertion of the dive.
- **Nausea.** Nausea is an ambiguous symptom without a direct cause related to bubble formation. It may, however, be the result of other symptoms indicating DCI, such as dizziness or vertigo.
- **Difficulty walking.** If a person has difficulty walking following a dive, it may be a sign of DCI.
- **Altered skin sensation.** Physical perceptions may be altered, and the person may have difficulty differentiating between objects that are sharp and dull, or soft and hard.

The preceding are the most common warning signs of DCI. The following are other possibilities:

- Rash and itching
- Difficulty breathing
- Visual disturbance
- Restlessness
- Paralysis
- Muscle twitching
- Unconsciousness

- Personality change
- Speech disturbance
- Altered level of responsiveness
- Bladder- or bowel-control problems
- Hearing loss or ringing in the ears
- Convulsions

Most signs and symptoms of DCI occur within the first two hours following a dive. Making an ascent to altitude (such as driving through the mountains or flying in an aircraft) following a dive may trigger symptoms or make them worse. Current recommendations for altitude exposure are as follows:

- **Single no-decompression dive.** A minimum surface interval of 12 hours is suggested.

- **Multiple dives per day or multiple days of diving.** A minimum surface interval of 18 hours is suggested (Sheffield and Vann, 2002).

Unfortunately, Divers Alert Network (DAN) statistics indicate that divers often don't call DAN or ask for help at the first sign of DCI. They call only when their symptoms don't go away. DAN statistics also show that divers wait an average of 17 hours after symptom onset before calling DAN or seeking definitive care. This delay makes it more difficult to treat DCI and lessens the likelihood of complete resolution of symptoms. Early symptom recognition is extremely important. If you suspect DCI in another diver, provide 100 percent emergency oxygen by mask and activate your emergency assistance plan (EAP), which should include contacting the DAN Emergency Hotline.

Benefits of Emergency Oxygen

Although the use of oxygen for non-diving injuries is beyond the scope of this book, there are many benefits to providing 100 percent oxygen to an injured diver when you believe his condition may be dive related. The nitrogen bubbles that form in the diver's body tissues and fluids can block blood flow and damage tissues.

When a person breathes 100 percent oxygen, the partial pressure of inspired oxygen increases, causing a pressure gradient between the inspired gas (oxygen) and the gas dissolved in the tissues (nitrogen). As a result, there is more nitrogen in the tissues than in the breathing gas, which increases the nitrogen elimination or off-gassing. Since excess nitrogen in the tissues and in bubbles in circulation causes decompression sickness, the elimination of nitrogen through off-gassing will have a beneficial effect. In some cases, providing 100 percent emergency oxygen has significantly improved or even completely resolved symptoms. However, this does not mean the diver is cured. The injured diver still requires definitive care at a specialized treatment facility or recompression chamber.

Emergency oxygen first aid may do the following:

- Increase the pressure gradient from the bubble to the surrounding tissues to allow for a more efficient elimination of nitrogen
- Increase oxygen levels in hypoxic tissue
- Reduce tissue swelling as a result of the reversing of the hypoxic process and because oxygen is a mild vasoconstrictor
- Ease breathing, in some cases
- Partially or completely resolve symptoms (This is the result of a greater concentration of oxygen being distributed throughout the body, minimizing the effect of a blockage. Typically, when the oxygen is removed, those symptoms reappear. Even if symptoms do resolve completely, the injured diver needs evaluation at an appropriate medical facility by a health care professional who is familiar with dive medicine.)
- Reduce the risk of residual symptoms after hyperbaric treatment

Emergency Oxygen Delivery

An emergency oxygen unit should include a cylinder with enough oxygen to treat at least one diver for the amount of time it takes to go from the dive site to the closest emergency medical services (EMS) location. It should also include a regulator to deliver the gas from the cylinder to a mask. We recommend three delivery methods for emergency oxygen first aid: the DAN demand inhalator valve, the nonrebreather mask, and the delivery of supplemental oxygen during CPR via a resuscitation mask.

Demand Inhalator Valve We recommend that oxygen units come equipped with a demand inhalator valve (see figure 11.4) such as the one found in the DAN emergency oxygen unit. A demand inhalator valve delivers the highest concentration of oxygen possible. It delivers oxygen only when the diver inhales, much like a scuba regulator, extending the duration of the oxygen cylinder. All DAN emergency oxygen units come with a multifunction regulator capable of delivering oxygen by demand inhalator valve, as well as free-flow devices such as the nonrebreather mask and resuscitation devices such as a rescue mask or a bag-valve mask.

Whenever you are at a dive location, your emergency oxygen unit should be completely assembled and ready for rapid deployment. Once you have determined that the diver

FIGURE 11.4 The demand inhalator valve provides a high concentration of inspired oxygen without any waste. Like a scuba regulator, it supplies oxygen only when the diver inhales.

needs emergency oxygen first aid, turn on the oxygen pressure and provide emergency oxygen using the most appropriate mask and delivery system. The demand inhalator valve should be your primary delivery device for injured divers who are breathing on their own. The demand inhalator valve will, with a good mask seal, provide as close to 100 percent inspired oxygen as possible.

Test the oxygen flow by inhaling from the mask and exhaling away from the mask before you give it to the injured diver. This reassures the diver that it is just oxygen and won't hurt him; it also confirms that oxygen is flowing. Place the mask over the injured diver's mouth and nose, and have him breathe normally. Ask the diver to hold the demand inhalator valve, relax, and breathe normally. If the diver can't tolerate the demand inhalator valve or is breathing so weakly they he cannot activate it, switch the injured diver to the nonrebreather mask.

Nonrebreather Mask When a demand inhalator valve isn't appropriate or when you have multiple injured divers and only one demand inhalator valve, multifunction oxygen regulators can provide a constant flow alternative. Some basic emergency oxygen units may have a constant flow regulator that can only deliver oxygen to an injured diver using a nonrebreather mask (see figure 11.5). This mask works well and is simple to use. However, because it is difficult to get a perfect mask seal, you are unlikely to get close to the 100 percent inspired oxygen that would provide the greatest benefit to the injured diver. Also, this device wastes oxygen gas because the oxygen flows even when the diver isn't inhaling.

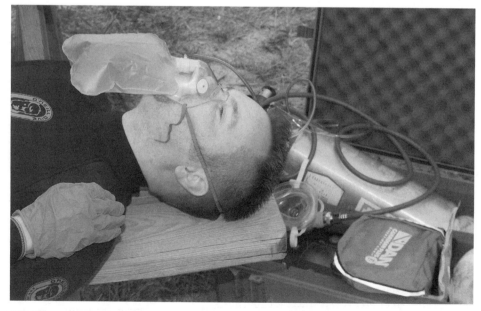

FIGURE 11.5 The nonrebreather mask delivers a high concentration of oxygen, but rescuers who use it must be vigilant about securing and maintaining the mask seal to keep the oxygen from being diluted.

The oxygen tubing is attached to the constant flow barbed outlet on the regulator. Before putting the nonrebreather mask over the diver's mouth and nose, set the flow rate at 15 liters per minute and place a gloved finger over the one-way valve leading to the mask's reservoir bag to fill it up. When using the nonrebreather mask, you should continually monitor the diver and the oxygen supply. Don't let the oxygen supply run out, or turn off the oxygen, when the mask is on the diver's face.

Supplemental Oxygen Delivery When delivering rescue breaths as part of CPR, you can supplement your efforts by connecting the oxygen supply to the rescue mask you are using to deliver the breaths, if the mask has an oxygen inlet (see figure 11.6). To do this, remove the oxygen tubing from the nonrebreather mask and connect it to the barbed constant flow outlet on the multifunction regulator, then connect the other end of the clear plastic tubing to the

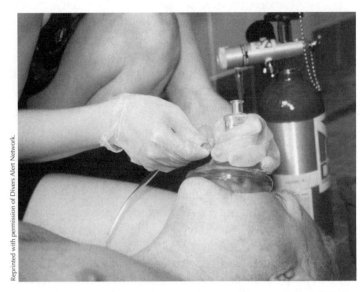

Reprinted with permission of Divers Alert Network.

FIGURE 11.6 Incorporating supplemental oxygen into CPR significantly raises the concentration of oxygen being delivered to the injured diver.

oxygen inlet on the rescue mask. Turn the oxygen flow to 15 liters per minute and continue delivering your breaths as normal. This raises your delivered oxygen concentration from 16 percent oxygen to approximately 50 percent.

Lung Overpressure

Rapid, shallow breathing; shortness of breath; or bluish skin, lips, and fingernails accompanied by chest pain may signal a lung overpressure injury. As mentioned previously, overpressure injuries are caused by gas expanding in the diver's lung during ascent. If the diver holds her breath or if for some other reason gas is trapped in the diver's lungs, damage to the lungs may result.

Mucus in the lungs can cause blockages that can trap air in the lungs that will expand on ascent. So, don't dive with a cold or congestion. And remember, even though you no longer feel any stuffiness, the cold may not have entirely passed. It typically takes about two weeks for a cold to completely clear your system and for your lungs to return to their normal functional level. There have been cases in which divers have coughed during ascent and provoked lung injuries.

Divers should not smoke. In a recent article in *Alert Diver* magazine, Dr. James Caruso, a forensic pathologist, wrote: "I am constantly reminded of the negative impact cigarette smoking has on an individual's health. From a medical viewpoint, it's difficult to imagine why anyone engaging in an activity like scuba diving, where efficient gas exchange and proper oxygenation of tissue play such an integral role, would smoke. Smoking can and does interfere with this exchange" (Caruso, 2004, p. 42).

Carbon monoxide, delivered through inhaled cigarette smoke, binds to the body's red blood cells and impairs their ability to deliver oxygen to body tissues. That fact alone should be enough to discourage divers from smoking. But, even worse, smoking impairs the body's ability to move mucus and other foreign bodies up and out of the airway. "This contributes greatly to the development of chronic bronchitis; it is also the main reason for 'smoker's cough' and the fact that longtime smokers bring up abundant secretions after sleeping. Irritation of the airways may also predispose the smoking diver to episodes of acute bronchospasm. A diver experiencing this phenomenon would have an increased risk for pulmonary barotrauma and gas embolism," Caruso explained (2004, p. 42).

If you believe a diver has a lung expansion injury, whatever the cause, you should initiate your emergency assistance plan and get the diver on a high concentration of oxygen. A lung injury may allow bubbles to enter the arterial circulation, as noted in our discussion of arterial gas embolism. Also, the diver's lungs may be severely damaged by overexpansion, which may in turn lead to lung collapse. Obviously a collapsed lung would impair the diver's ability to breathe, and hypoxia could result. Recompression may not be indicated for a diver with some lung injuries, but evacuation may be recommended.

Other Medical Problems

There are several other medical problems to consider. Although divers are not any more likely to have a heart attack while diving than while participating in other outdoor recreational activities, we tend to dive in places where medical care is harder to access. For this reason we need to be prepared to handle emergencies on our own. Adequate preparation requires a good emergency assistance plan and information that goes beyond what is taught in basic first aid and CPR programs. Generally, those programs are based on the idea that emergency medical services can respond within 10 minutes. Such a rapid response is simply not feasible in most of the popular remote dive locations.

Cardiac Problems

If the conscious person has what appears to be a cardiac-related condition, you should provide any medications he may be taking for the condition, support his airway and breathing, and arrange for transport or emergency medical help. You can also give the person emergency oxygen first aid. If he is not showing any signs of breathing, perform CPR and use an AED. Aside from these basics, there isn't much more you can do from a first aid perspective. Advanced life support from trained healthcare professionals (EMS providers) is essential.

Although cardiac arrest can come on without warning, cardiac problems may produce signs or symptoms such as the following:

- Heavy pressure or squeezing pain or discomfort in the center of the chest behind the breastbone
- Shoulder, arm, neck, or jaw pain, frequently radiating to the left arm
- Extreme fatigue
- Shortness of breath
- Sweating
- Nausea and vomiting
- Denial or minimization of the seriousness of the situation

If you see these signs or experience these symptoms yourself, especially when there is no obvious reason for them, you should immediately suspect cardiac problems until proven otherwise. The moment you believe a diver may be having cardiac-related trouble, you need to initiate care and start the process of getting the diver to medical help.

Diabetes

For years insulin-requiring diabetes has been a medical concern for diving. For just as many years, divers with insulin-dependent or insulin-requiring diabetes have been diving regularly. Initial DAN research, based on a series of anonymous surveys, indicated that many divers with diabetes had been diving for many years. In 2005, after several years of studying divers with diabetes, Divers Alert Network released a report called *Diabetes and Recreational Diving: Guidelines for the Future* that included several recommendations (Pollock, Uguccioni, and Dear, 2005). These recommendations are simply guidelines to help diabetic divers regulate their blood sugar levels. However, even if a diver has followed these guidelines strictly, the diver and anyone diving with him must be cautious and prepared to manage a diabetes-related emergency.

Obviously, a diver with diabetes should assess his own fitness to dive, just as any diver should do. He should ask himself, "Do I feel ready to dive? Do I feel well?" While gearing up and preparing for the dive, the diver should complete a minimum of three blood glucose tests to see whether his glucose level is stable or is trending upward or downward. Predive glucose tests should be done an hour before the dive, half an hour before the dive, and immediately prior to the dive. The diver's blood glucose level should be at least 150 and stable or rising before he enters the water. If it is less than 150, he should delay the dive until his glucose level has increased.

For self-rescue, a diabetic diver should carry oral glucose in a readily accessible location while underwater during all dives. He should also have parenteral glucagon available at the surface. If a diabetic diver or his buddy notices hypoglycemia while underwater, the diabetic diver should make a controlled ascent to the surface, make himself positively buoyant, and ingest his oral glucose. He should then leave the water and continually monitor his blood sugar level.

A diver with diabetes who notices no problems during the dive should still check his blood sugar regularly for 12 to 15 hours after diving and keep himself hydrated. Also, he should make sure to log all of his dives and include all blood glucose information as well to help him manage his levels in the future.

There are two possible medical conditions associated with diabetes to be concerned about. The first is an insulin reaction, which occurs when a diver's blood sugar is out of control. He may demonstrate altered mental status and shocklike conditions. He may be weak and uncoordinated if he is responsive. He may also have a rapid pulse and may possibly have a seizure. If you notice a diver exhibiting any of these signs, immediately give him sugar or glucose and monitor him for any additional problems if he is conscious and in control of his airway.

A much more serious condition is a diabetic coma. Some of the signs of an impending diabetic coma include headache and thirst with excessive urination. The diver may be dehydrated with warm and dry skin. He may also have a deep sighing breath with a fruity odor and complain of not feeling well for days. There is very little you can do for a diver experiencing a diabetic coma in the field. Your only options are to keep him comfortable; support his airway, breathing, and circulation; and get him to advanced life support as quickly as you can.

A diabetic diver may or may not have a MedicAlert bracelet or other medical tag. Divers with diabetes or any other medical condition should always inform their buddy of the condition and discuss how best to manage the situation if a problem were to occur before, during, or after the dive. Diving with medical conditions such as diabetes can present unique challenges for the diver and his companions. Therefore, a diver with such a condition should seek competent and qualified medical advice before entering or continuing the sport.

Thermal Stress and Related Illnesses

Thermal stress occurs when a diver is exposed to heat or cold and results in significant changes in the diver's core temperature. Either an increase (hyperthermia) or a decrease (hypothermia) in core temperature can cause serious safety concerns for the diver. Even mild thermal variations could have serious safety consequences because they can cause predive preparation or planning errors or make a diver inattentive during the dive.

Hyperthermia Hyperthermia may manifest itself in a variety of conditions including heat stress, heat exhaustion, and heat stroke. Recognizing and addressing early-stage hyperthermia can prevent it from progressing to a more dangerous condition.

- **Heat stress and heat exhaustion.** Heat stress can be a problem, even when diving in cold water. Getting suited up (dry- or wetsuit) on a hot summer day, or in a poorly ventilated space such as on board a dive boat, can create heat stress leading to mistakes in planning and preparation and other heat-related issues. Mild heat stress may not be considered a serious condition by some divers, but it can become serious very quickly if the symptoms aren't addressed.

The signs and symptoms of heat exhaustion include a rapid pulse, dizziness, anxiety, irritability, headache, and visual disturbances. The diver will also display normal to slightly elevated body temperatures, but have pale, cool, and sweaty skin. She may also have mild cramps, nausea, and vomiting. Heat stress may be precipitated by vomiting, diarrhea, and other conditions that lead to dehydration such as predive alcohol intake.

Heat stress can also cause a diver to make mistakes in dive planning and equipment preparation. Therefore, you should prepare your dive equipment before you don your exposure protection. Remember that heat stress can exacerbate other conditions in diving such as seasickness, so it is best to stay as cool as you can for as long as you can.

Obviously, the best option for managing heat stress in a diving situation is to stop it before it becomes a problem. Divers should keep well-hydrated during equipment preparation and all predive activities. If the potential for heat stress exists, you should attempt to remain cool while donning your exposure protection. If you are wearing a wetsuit, you should either get it wet before putting it on, or don it in steps. For example, put on your wetsuit boots and pants and then get wet. Once you are comfortable, you can take the next step and put on your jacket and hood. There isn't much you can do to cool off when using a drysuit. You can keep the zipper open to allow some air circulation, but make sure it is closed all the way as part of your predive equipment check. If you have gotten uncomfortable and can't cool off, you can call the dive. Remember the cardinal rule in diving safety: *anyone can call a dive for any reason—even before it starts.*

If you are aiding a diver with heat exhaustion, keep her calm and cool her off slowly. Get her out of the heat, into the shade or into air conditioning. If she is conscious and having no trouble breathing, you can give her fluids to help rehydrate her. Side effects of dehydration are low blood pressure and low blood concentration. By rehydrating, you reverse both conditions. Dehydration can also exacerbate a variety of conditions, including DCI.

Water is the preferred fluid for rehydration, but sport drinks such as Gatorade are specially formulated, often with electrolytes, to aid in rehydration. A common misconception is that sport drinks should be diluted with water, but there is no scientific validity to that notion. Have the diver drink normally. Do not attempt to force additional fluids, and discourage the diver from drinking too quickly because doing so may cause vomiting.

- **Heat stroke.** Heat stroke is a very serious medical condition and, if it is not treated quickly and effectively, it can cause death. Heat stroke is a situation in which a person's body heat has risen beyond the body's ability to regulate it. A diver suffering from heat stroke will have a rapid pulse and red, hot, dry skin. These symptoms may not be as evident in people who are physically fit, as a fit body is better able to compensate for the stressors. The diver may also have a headache and exhibit weakness, dizziness, anxiety, or fatigue. She will probably not be sweating at this point.

◣ Orr's Safety Stop: Heat Dangers

Sometimes members of a diving party are so focused on what is happening in the water and keeping the divers safe that they forget to take equal care of our surface support people. A number of years ago we were doing course training for an upcoming advanced-level dive. The last weekend in June was hot and humid, as only June in Ohio can get. Our surface support team was helping the divers get geared up quickly and correctly, and getting them into the water so that they wouldn't get over-heated in their wetsuits. Running back and forth for forgotten equipment, lifting tanks off the beach and onto waiting divers, recording entry times—the surface support team was busy doing everything but noticing that the air temperature was topping 100 degrees (45 °C).

All the students had completed their entries when one of the members of the support team finally sat down. She noticed that her skin was hot and dry to the touch and that she was feeling lightheaded. Before she could say anything to the other members of the surface support team, she passed out. When she came to, she was looking straight up at that very clear, blue sky. For a moment, before the other team members rushed to her aid, she thought she had gone blind.

Emergency medical services was just down the road. By the time they reached the site, the woman was already sitting up and feeling woozy. They checked her vital signs, determined that it was heat exhaustion, and recommended that she get out of the sun and into a cool location, drink plenty of fluids, sit out from the rest of the day's activities, and have one of the other staff check on her periodically. A diver who later came up out of the water walked up to the recuperating woman as she sat in the shade and told her she looked really pale and that she should get out in the sun and get a little color. What she said in return, although instructional, does not bear repeating. This experience illustrates the need to keep both diving and surface personnel comfortable and to watch out for signs of thermal stress.

Heat stroke requires aggressive intervention. You should alert the authorities and activate your emergency assistance plan. You must rapidly lower the diver's body core temperature. Remove her clothing and cover her with a cool, water-soaked blanket. Get her into air conditioning if it is available. You will also need to give her emergency oxygen and support her airway and breathing. To aid in cooling, you can also place cold packs in her armpits and groin and along her head and neck to keep her cool. You should be prepared for convulsions. EMS providers may give the diver intravenous fluids, but they shouldn't use fluids that contain dextrose, such as D5W. Dextrose can contribute to edema or increased production of lactic acid, leading to poor outcome in the event of a neurological injury.

Hypothermia Hypothermia is the loss of body heat caused by exposure to cold or inadequate thermal protection. Cold stress can cause inattentiveness and loss of concentration resulting in predive preparation and planning errors. Although water conducts heat away from the body 20 to 27 times faster than air, divers can also experience cold stress when exposed to cold air temperatures before a dive.

Anytime divers are exposed to cold water, you should be prepared to deal with hypothermia. When diving in cold water, or making long dives in cool water, keep an eye on the divers in your group and be aware of any indication of trouble. Divers focused on underwater tasks can get mildly hypothermic before they even realize it. Remember, even 80-degree (27 °C) "tropical" water is still nearly 20 degrees (10 °C) colder than normal body temperature. If any diver in your group exhibits possible signs of hypothermia, treat him as though hypothermia is present.

As with heat stress, there are levels of cold stress. Divers can move quickly from mild to moderate to severe hypothermia if early symptoms, such as sluggishness and slowed motor skills, are ignored. Early recognition of mild problems and quick intervention into those problems can keep them from becoming more serious.

MUSCLE CRAMPS

Cold water and exertion can cause muscle cramps. Before you get in the water, whether it is a warm or cold water dive, and especially after a period of diving inactivity, you should stretch properly. Although all divers learn how to release a cramp on their own in their initial training (by grabbing their fin tip and pulling backward), you should practice this skill regularly. If you have a serious muscle cramp, don't hesitate to signal your buddy for help. Your buddy can help you release a cramp quickly. It may not even interfere with the dive. However, a cramp left unattended could eventually lead to an inability to swim, a loss of buoyancy, or getting separated from a buddy. If you experience a cramp early in the dive, you and your buddy may elect to stay near the entry or exit point instead of committing yourself to a long swim.

- **Mild hypothermia.** Mild hypothermia is classified as anytime the body's core temperature drops to 95 °F (35 °C). The diver will be shivering and apathetic. He may have difficulty with motor skills including a wobbling gait and awkward manual control. He may also appear confused or forgetful. Mild hypothermia can occur even in relatively warm, tropical waters, and it is not safe for the diver to continue to dive in this state.

- **Moderate hypothermia.** Should the diver's condition move beyond mild hypothermia, the diver's shivering will stop as the diver's body core temperature dips to 88 °F (31 °C). The diver will be stuporous, and his heartbeat and respirations will have slowed down. His pupils may be dilated. Moderate hypothermia is a serious and potentially life-threatening condition, and the diver needs immediate care and rewarming.

- **Severe hypothermia.** At this point, the diver's core temperature will be nearly 80 °F (27 °C). All of his voluntary responses will be gone, as well as most of his reflexes. This is a life-threatening condition requiring immediate treatment.

Since there is no way to accurately assess the diver's core temperature, you have to look for obvious signs of hypothermia. Bluish coloration of the lips and uncontrolled shivering should indicate that the diver is in no condition to embark on or continue with a dive. In this situation, it's best to abort the dive and restore normal body temperature when the diver is safely out of the water. Even mildly hypothermic divers are likely to experience a loss in coordination and muscle strength as well as some degree of mental confusion. Any of these conditions are certainly incompatible with safe diving.

The best method for rewarming a diver in hypothermia will vary depending on the available equipment, support, and the other conditions that require treatment at the same time. You also have to balance two priorities: minimizing afterdrop and maximizing rewarming.

Afterdrop is a problem that occurs when the colder blood in the extremities moves to the body core during rewarming, causing the core temperature to drop. This rapid drop in the body's core temperature during the rewarming process can actually cause the diver's condition to deteriorate further. Monitor the diver carefully to make sure he continues to improve.

To begin the rewarming process, you need to prevent any further heat loss. Remove any wet clothing and get the diver dried off. Be sure to rewarm the diver slowly and in a warm environment so he can also warm from the inside out. Always handle a hypothermic diver gently. Rough handling can bring on worsening symptoms including cardiac arrest as cold blood rushes to the heart. When caring for the diver, you should maintain his airway and breathing. If CPR is necessary, rewarm the diver while doing compressions. Medical experts generally don't consider someone dead until he has first been warmed up.

Divers with moderate to severe hypothermia will need more aggressive warming strategies. These include heat packs at the head, neck, armpits, and groin, along with warm-water baths. On a boat, you can get warm water from the engine or compressor cooling system. Have someone who is not cold

PREVENTING HYPOTHERMIA

If you realize you are shivering uncontrollably, you should immediately abort the dive and get out of the water. There is nothing you can do to conserve or generate much heat underwater. Remember, the loss of fine motor control skills and grip strength may result in difficulty releasing your weights, grasping your inflator hose, gripping a ladder or providing assistance to a buddy in distress.

If you are floating on the surface in cold water and are separated from the rest of the divers or your boat, make yourself as buoyant as possible and remain still. Curl up in the fetal position and assume the Heat Escape Lessening Posture (HELP). Drownproofing by lying face down in the water to float and only raising the head out of the water to breathe is not recommended in cold water because of the associated heat loss through the head and neck. If others are nearby, huddle together to conserve heat; this will also help you keep yourselves calm.

determine the correct water temperature. Remember to be as gentle with the diver as you can. During transport, keep the diver's head above the heart.

Some common misconceptions exist about how to warm a hypothermic person. Placing the extremities in a warm-water bath has not been shown to make much difference. Skin-to-skin heat donation, in which the hypothermic person is placed inside a sleeping bag with a rescuer, doesn't transfer very much heat either. It also takes away a potential rescuer. Although drinking warm fluids may make the diver feel better, it really doesn't, by itself, result in significant rewarming because the diver can only ingest so much fluid. Generally, a combination of approaches does the most good—providing hot liquids, allowing the diver to breathe warm air, and adding warm blankets or clothes. If you are able to get the diver to medical help quickly, you may want to consider delaying rewarming. Medical professionals have more sophisticated and efficient ways of warming the body from the inside out.

Head-to-Toe Secondary Survey

It is entirely possible that you will not have the opportunity to move beyond providing basic life support to perform a secondary survey. Only after the diver is stabilized and there is time prior to evacuation should you consider attempting to gain additional information. If these circumstances apply and the diver is injured or complaining of an illness, perform a secondary assessment to determine the extent of the problem and to see if other problems exist. Examine the diver's body, focusing on areas of trauma or complaint.

During the secondary survey, you use your eyes and hands to recognize abnormalities. Before starting the physical examination, take a moment to protect yourself. Don appropriate barrier devices. You don't want to come in contact with blood or other bodily fluids accidentally.

To begin, you will need to remove any unnecessary clothing, including cutting away the wetsuit. As you remove the clothes, begin scanning the body. At this point, start feeling at the head for deformities and watch for blood or other fluids. Note any reaction to your touch. You should also scan the diver's ears for blood or any fluid. From there, slide your hands down her neck. Attempt to determine the mechanism of injury so that you can assess whether a head or neck injury is likely. A neck injury is considered unlikely unless the diver has been hit by a boat or was attempting a head-first entry into the water. However, you may be called upon to perform a secondary survey on a diver who fell from a boat or was hit by a falling piece of equipment.

Move in front of the diver and shade her eyes from the sun. Do this one eye at a time to see if they dilate in response. Scan the diver's face with your fingertips to determine whether there are any broken bones underneath the skin. You should also check the diver's nostrils for blood or fluid discharge. Have the diver open her mouth, or open it for her, and look for any problems inside including dislodged teeth, debris, or clots. You can remove them if they are easily accessible, but be careful to avoid forcing them in farther.

Feel the front of the neck for swelling, which may indicate air bubbles. Listen for a crackling sound from underneath the skin. This could indicate subcutaneous emphysema, which is caused by air bubbles escaping from the lungs and chest cavity and moving under the skin in the neck, upper chest, or back. Although this is an emergency in and of itself, it may be associated with other trauma and injury to the lungs caused by lung overexpansion.

Next, scan the diver's collarbone for injuries or discoloration. Press your fingers gently along each collarbone individually. If you examine both at the same time, and the diver reacts, you may not be able to tell which is the affected side.

Moving down, reexamine the diver's torso (see figure 11.7a). You should note any open wounds. If you see blood bubbling in the chest region, apply direct pressure to the wound to stop air from moving in and out. If there are no obvious open wounds, hold one side of the chest while you press along the other searching for broken ribs.

Divide the abdomen into four quadrants. Press gently but firmly on each quadrant in turn to check for any areas that are sensitive, stiff, hard, or painful (see figure 11.7b). Identify and note the location of any abnormalities using the terms upper left quadrant, lower left quadrant, upper right quadrant, or lower right quadrant (always referring to the diver's left or right and not your own).

Continuing downward, place a hand on either side of the diver's pelvis and push the sides together and down, as if pressing the pelvis into the ground. Note any instability or painful response.

Finally, examine the arms and legs (see figure 11.7c), pushing hard enough to feel the bones beneath the skin and muscle. Immobilize the arms and legs by holding the diver at the ankle and wrist and ask her to wiggle her fingers and toes.

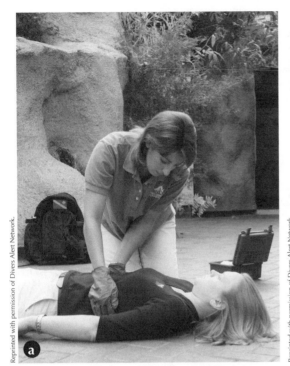

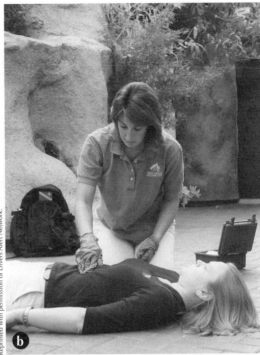

Reprinted with permission of Divers Alert Network.

Reprinted with permission of Divers Alert Network.

Reprinted with permission of Divers Alert Network.

FIGURE 11.7 When conducting a secondary survey to check for additional injuries, begin at the diver's head, scanning for bleeding or other fluids. As you work down the body, check the chest for open wounds and *(a)* search for broken ribs. Then *(b)* scan the torso, looking for abnormalities or bleeding. Finally, *(c)* scan the diver's arms and legs.

As part of your information gathering, you should record the diver's pulse rate and breathing rate. Also, you will want to record a medical history using the acronym SAMPLE. This reflects the following:

Signs and symptoms
Allergies
Medications
Past illnesses or injuries
Last meal or oral intake
Events leading up to current situation

PART III

Special Environments and Situations

12

Currents and Dams

Sometimes the biggest problem on a dive is the water itself—at least when the water is working against you. Divers often end up exhausting themselves trying to swim against a current, and then they get in trouble. The best plan for dealing with a current is to avoid it in the first place. Before you make a dive or try out a new dive site, gather as much information as possible about the site, including currents and waves, potential trouble spots such as dams or water intakes in freshwater lakes and rivers, as well as any other features important for safety.

Currents and Drifting

In general, currents are a part of diving in the ocean. Occasionally, currents are an issue in freshwater, such as in a river or a lake the size of the Great Lakes. They shouldn't necessarily make you change your mind about a dive, however; you just need to be prepared to deal with them.

When diving at a site where a strong current is running across the surface, divers should always use a descent line or the anchor line to get to the bottom (see figure 12.1). As noted in chapter 1, you may need to use a swim line from the stern or entry point to the anchor line or descent line to keep from exhausting yourself swimming against the current before the dive has even begun. Once on the bottom, take a few seconds to assess the direction of the current, as it may be different compared to the surface, and then swim into the current. The boat crew should trail a line with a float (a life ring or other buoyant object) behind the boat (known as a trail line; see figure 12.2), so that

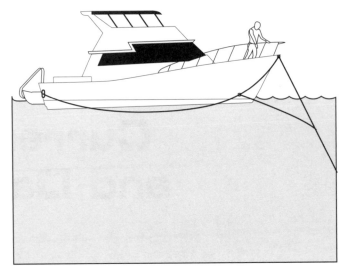

FIGURE 12.1 When diving from a boat in current, use swim lines and descent lines to move from the entry point to the dive site.

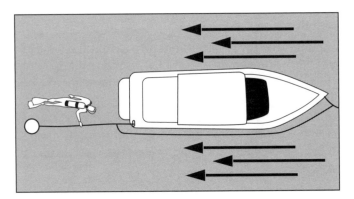

FIGURE 12.2 A trail line allows divers who are waiting to enter the boat to stay close to the boat without having to fight a surface current.

divers who are waiting to exit up the boat ladder are not swept away by the current. A trail line can also help divers who ascend away from the boat; they can swim to the line and pull themselves back to the boat. The anchor line or descent line can be used to facilitate safety stops or obligatory decompression stops. Some vessels have weighted PVC pipes at 10 to 15 feet (3 to 4.6 meters) to facilitate these stops.

If you will be descending using lines, the boat crew should include related procedures as part of your dive briefing, explaining the specific details of how the boat is set up and how the lines are rigged. As soon as you have returned to the surface after making your entry into the water, grab the swim line and hold on while you wait for your buddy and prepare to make the dive. You will want to move out of the way to allow other divers to enter the water.

Remember, it is important to keep your regulator in your mouth from the time you enter the water until you are back on the boat at the end of the dive.

Inexperienced divers occasionally will switch to their snorkels while on the surface. This technique is not advised in the open water since it leaves you vulnerable to waves higher than the length of your snorkel. Also, if you must provide assistance to a diving companion, you don't want to waste valuable time trying to switch to your regulator at a moment of crisis.

Use your hands to pull yourself along the swim line to where it meets the descent line or anchor line, pause there long enough to make sure your diving companions are with you, and then begin your descent. If you anticipate any trouble clearing your ears during descent, you may want to switch to a head-up orientation and descend feet first. When you arrive on the bottom, pay close attention to the direction and speed of the current. Remember, though, that currents can shift and the dive may lead you in another direction, making the swim back more difficult.

In some places with fast-running currents, dive operations may plan dives as drift dives, in which the boat follows the divers as they drift along with the current. The divers and the boat captain need to be experienced and prepared for this type of diving. All the divers should remain together during the entire dive and during the ascent. Remember, the current may be traveling at different speeds at different depths. Divers need to carry signaling devices (this should be a standard part of their dive equipment) to alert the dive boat of their location. In addition, all divers in the party need to be familiar with the drift diving process, which includes staying together, ascending together, and performing a safety stop while drifting.

If you surface from a dive and find that you have been carried away from the boat by a current, you should blow your whistle, yell, wave, or slap the water to get attention. You can also use a safety sausage (see figure 12.3) or other surface signaling device, such as a mirror during the day or a cyalume stick at night, to let the boat know you need help and to make it easier for them to find you. If possible, attach your cyalume stick to the upper portion of your safety sausage, so that you can be seen more easily from a distance.

FIGURE 12.3 When you surface away from the dive boat, deploy a safety sausage to make yourself more visible. Doing so is especially important when waves or currents are present because they can pull you away from the boat and can hinder the boat crew's ability to see you.

Remember, don't wear yourself out fighting a current. Under the best circumstances, divers can swim only about one mile (1.6 kilometers) per hour for any prolonged period. Currents can far exceed that speed. You cannot even maintain your position, much less make headway, against swift-moving water.

If you must attempt to swim against a current on the surface, make yourself horizontal in the water to minimize drag. You can make yourself buoyant by inflating your BCD, but inflate it only as much as necessary to stay at the surface. A fully inflated BCD creates drag, making it harder to swim. Remember from the introduction of this book that doubling your surface area means that it will take four times as much energy to move through the water at the same speed. Anything you do that presents a larger profile against the water makes swimming harder. Also, a fully inflated BCD can put pressure on your chest, making it more difficult to breathe. You may find it easier to swim on your back, but doing so can make it more difficult to watch where you are going and to swim in a straight line. Because one leg is naturally stronger than the other, you could end up swimming in circles.

You may need to drop items you are carrying if they are restricting your ability to swim. Consider swimming to the shore or another nearby vessel and have the boat pick you up there, if that would be easier. If you still have air in your tank and are in relatively shallow water, consider going back underwater where the currents may be weaker in order to make better headway. You can pull yourself along the bottom if the currents are still strong. If you have a compass, take a heading, follow the bottom profile, or gain some other bearing so you can navigate to the boat or shore.

If the boat has to come to get you, you and your dive buddy or companions should stay together, relax, and wait. If the boat doesn't have a small craft that can be put in the water to come to get you, make yourself buoyant and float until help arrives. If you float along with the current, the boat should be able to follow you easily. The boat crew will need to recall all the other divers and account for each of them before raising the anchor, so don't panic. Keep your diving companions with you and do everything you can to be seen once the boat is underway to come and get you.

Once all the other divers are on board and you have been spotted, the boat should approach you in the water cautiously. The propellers should be in neutral or the engines shut off before it gets close. The boat crew should throw you a float attached to a line so they can pull you toward the boat.

Rip and Longshore Currents

When you are making a dive from shore, you must be aware of rapid movements of water offshore called rip currents. Rip currents are rapid currents that move perpendicular to the beach (see figure 12.4). They occur when water from waves rushes back to sea through a narrow channel between

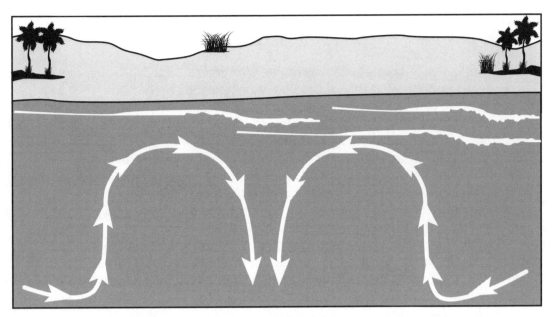

FIGURE 12.4 A rip current is created when waves are funneled out through a single exit pathway on the sand, creating a fast-moving current that runs perpendicular to the beach. Even experienced divers must respect the power of a rip current, and act accordingly.

reefs, sandbars, or shoreline configurations. Rip currents can move from 3 to 12 miles (5 to 19 kilometers) per hour, far exceeding the aforementioned speed of 1 mile (1.6 kilometers) per hour that a fully equipped diver, even in the best physical shape, can attain. A rip current is generally identifiable by the cloudy or discolored water or foam moving away from the beach. Surf will also be low or absent in that area, making it appear to be a natural spot for divers to attempt an exit.

There are some who say you can use a rip current to your advantage to quickly get offshore. Limited visibility and rapid water movement may make using a rip current less than desirable. If you are caught in a rip current, the simplest way to get out is to swim parallel to the beach. This moves you across the rip current and possibly out of harm's way. Once you move outside of the flow, you can swim in. If you get caught in a rip tide at the beginning of your dive, you and your buddy may want to continue moving parallel to the shoreline to position yourselves away from the rip current area.

Unlike rip currents, longshore currents run parallel to the beach (see figure 12.5). You will have to swim through the longshore current to get out to your intended offshore dive site. To get back to shore, swim at a right angle to the current, or directly at the shore. If you need to reach a specific dive site offshore or to exit from the water at a specific point, swim diagonally against the current. If the longshore current is especially strong, you may need to descend to the bottom and pull yourself in the intended direction.

◼ Orr's Safety Stop: Current Dangers

On a trip to the Gulf coast of Florida, we planned to do a few beach dives at a popular site near a rock jetty. The only currents we had heard of were those flowing through the channel inside the jetty, caused by predictable tidal flows and a gentle longshore current running parallel to the beach. Just to be on the safe side, we decided to talk with a local dive operator about the site and water conditions. Everything appeared to be as we had been told, with one exception: The local weather reports indicated the possibility of wind and rain the day of our planned shore dive.

The morning of the dive, the onshore winds were pretty strong, causing some pretty impressive surf. We quickly made the decision not to attempt a scuba dive, but the surf looked inviting. We were just going to do a little body surfing—*what harm could come to us if we were positively buoyant and just a few yards from shore?* Being relatively inexperienced, we did not know enough about surf and current conditions to really understand and appreciate the risks.

We decided to don our wetsuits (without mask, snorkel, and fins) and play in the surf. Almost immediately, we were caught in a tremendously strong rip current that was pulling us offshore. This particular rip current was caused by the strong winds pushing water along the shore toward the jetty. Once the water reached the jetty, it was forced offshore. When we realized what was happening, we tried to swim across the rip current (in this case, away from the jagged rocks of the jetty), but that caused us to swim against the wind and into ever-increasing wave action.

We then decided to reverse ourselves and swim back toward the jetty, but by that time the rip current had taken us out past the end of the jetty. Under normal conditions, we would probably have been able to reach the point where the rip current was beginning to dissipate and we could have begun to make our way back to shore. Unfortunately, the wind and waves pushed us into the tidal current that was flowing out of the jetty, and we were forced even farther offshore.

To make matters worse, the wind and waves had increased significantly, and our partners on the beach were unable to get anyone to come to our aid because of the increasingly dangerous state of the sea. Even though we were positively buoyant, we were being tumbled around by the waves and having difficulty keeping water out of our mouths and noses. I thought we were going to drown on the surface. I grabbed my partner and told him that we needed to stay together no matter what. Eventually, we were able to swim parallel to the shore and make progress against the winds and to get away from the currents, but for a while we thought we were doomed. The whole experience was an important lesson in respecting the power of nature.

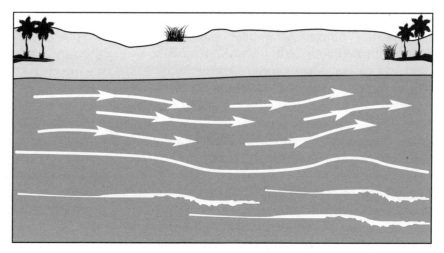

FIGURE 12.5   Longshore currents are fast moving flows that run parallel to the beach. They are often unavoidable but generally manageable.

Lowhead Dams

Lowhead dams are small dams in freshwater rivers with no spillway. They are used to slow the water flow in a small stream. The height of the dam has little to do with its danger. They can be as low as 12 inches (30.5 centimeters) and still be dangerous. As shown in figure 12.6, when the water flows over the dam, it sets up a boiling froth, or hydraulic, as the water falls over the dam and churns up on the bottom on the downstream side. It is possible to get too close to this hydraulic and be pulled into the recirculation toward the dam. Divers should never dive in or around lowhead dams.

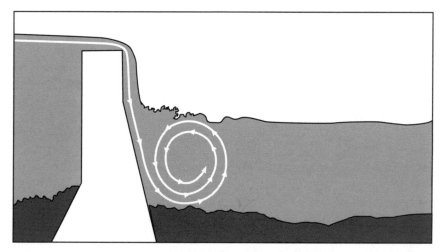

FIGURE 12.6   A lowhead dam is designed to slow the flow of water through a shallow stream. The boil immediately below the dam can be dangerous, as it can pull a diver into the recirculation cycle.

Once caught in the hydraulic of a lowhead dam, a diver will find it very difficult to extract himself. More often than not, the result is a body recovery. The force of the hydraulic pulls the diver toward the face of the dam, where he is forced underwater, only to pop up a short distance downstream. He is still in the current, however, and it will eventually pull him back to the dam face and back underwater, perpetuating the cycle. The power of the water far exceeds even the strongest person's ability to extricate himself from the situation.

If you do find yourself caught in the hydraulic of a lowhead dam, find a hard, steady surface handhold and signal for help. You can attempt to work your way to the side of the flow, where the pressure may be weaker, but you will likely need help to get out. Underwater, you should get to the bottom, grab onto whatever you can and work your way to the side. From there, you can try to make your way past and out of the hydraulic. This is not as easy as it sounds, though. The pressure of the recirculating water and the water falling

◣ Orr's Safety Stop: Rescuer Safety

I was teaching a course to a group of fire department rescue personnel who wanted to start a public service dive team. At my request, they agreed to demonstrate how they use a fire hose inflated with air to reach out to someone caught in a hydraulic. The positive buoyancy of the air-filled fire hose is sufficient to prevent it from being dragged underwater. The swimmer or boater can grab on to the hose and be pulled to safety without endangering the lives of the rescuers, who could also be caught in the hydraulic if they attempted to enter the water or make a rescue by boat.

When we arrived at the dam site for the demonstration, we became involved in a real-life rescue scenario. As we were preparing the fire hose for inflation, we noticed a couple of mallard ducks flapping furiously in the water just at the top of the spillway. Six ducklings had gone over the spillway and were caught in the hydraulic below. As each duckling was pulled into the face of the spillway, it was pulled underwater only to pop up a few yards downstream and be pulled toward the dam again.

One of the rescue team members said he thought he could wade out there and pull the ducklings to safety. This was a perfect demonstration of the kind of incorrect decision that could cost the lives of rescue personnel that we had been talking about in our course. Once this was pointed out, everyone recognized the folly of that option, and we set about using the skills and equipment we had at our disposal. We inflated the fire hose, moved it out into the hydraulic near the face of the spillway, and swept the six ducklings downstream and out of the effects of the hydraulic. Once the victims were safe, their parents flew downstream and moved the family farther downstream and out of harm's way. Lives were saved and an important lesson was learned by all (including the ducklings)!

from above can easily dislodge your regulator, pull your mask off, and pull you backward.

Never attempt to rescue a diver caught below a dam by going into the water after him. Leave that to the professionals. Get a line to the diver, preferably one with a float attached, and try to pull him out. If this does not work, tell the diver to inflate his BCD and hold onto something, and wait until the rescue squad arrives.

Unfortunately, sometimes even the professionals lack the specific training required to manage a rescue under these dangerous conditions, and the results can be tragic. Many years ago, fire department personnel attempted to rescue boaters caught in a hydraulic downstream from a lowhead dam only to have their boat capsize, putting them into the same situation. A second boat with more rescue personnel approached the scene only to be capsized as well. The tragic loss of life included the boaters and a number of rescue personnel. As a result of these and many other misguided rescue attempts, alternative measures were developed to save lives and reduce the risk to rescue personnel in such situations.

13

Overheads and Entanglements

Openwater divers who observe the basic techniques of diving—being fully trained and prepared for the dive environment—avoid diving in overhead environments without first acquiring the necessary specialized training, experience, and equipment. Anytime a diver can't make a direct vertical ascent to the surface and air, he is in an overhead environment. The diver might be under ice, in a cave, or penetrating a wreck. Or perhaps a virtual overhead condition exists. The diver might have an obligated decompression requirement, or be unable to ascend directly to the surface because of a dangerous surface condition such as boat traffic. Regardless of the reason, an inability to ascend directly to the surface presents a unique set of circumstances that require unique skills and training.

Getting entangled underwater is not a common occurrence, but when it does happen, it presents challenges that may significantly increase the stress on an unprepared diver. The most common thing divers become entangled in is fishing line, but they can also get caught up in kelp and, rarely, fishing nets around wrecks with poor visibility.

Diving in Overhead Environments

Any diver who is planning to dive in an overhead environment must have specialized training and equipment. Recreational open-water divers are not trained or prepared to make an ice, cavern, or cave dive or to do wreck penetration. Years of diving experience and advanced or even instructor credentials will not prepare you for all the unique challenges presented by overhead environments. Regardless of the reason for the dive, if you don't have the specialized training necessary to complete the dive safely—stay out.

Divers and rescuers need special training before diving in an overhead environment such as ice.

© Bruce Coleman

Just as a diver should not enter overhead environments without special training, neither should a rescuer. Such situations require specialized equipment and techniques. Although a diver can get into obligated decompression within recreational diving limits, many times when trouble occurs the diver is deeper than recommended and does not have the specialized training, experience, equipment, or sufficient gas to complete the decompression. Obviously, a search for a missing diver may require diving beyond recreational limits. Thus, a rescuer must be fully prepared to make a dive beyond the normal limits with minimal risk.

When diving beyond the realm of recreational diving, many standard safety practices apply, including the creation and use of a detailed dive plan and a rescue plan. Divers should never enter any overhead situation, virtual or otherwise, on a whim or enter a wreck or cave unprepared. In a recent dive fatality, the coroner determined that an experienced wreck diver and dive instructor had violated his own dive protocols. The violations, including entering a wreck without safety lines and entering into a portion of the wreck that was considered unsafe, led to his death (Rodgers, 2006).

In any overhead environment you should use the rule of thirds for your air or gas supply. Considering that it will take you at least as long to exit the dive as it did to enter it, you should plan your dive accordingly. The first third of your air supply is used to penetrate the wreck or cave system and conduct your search. Once you have reached that predetermined point, whether you have met your objective or not, it is time to turn around. That leaves you with a third of your air supply to exit and another full third to use for emergencies or to assist another diver. A point to consider, though, is that a diver who has made the mistake of using all of her air while still in an overhead situation is probably going to be panicked or at least contemplating her mortality. Fear may cause her to breathe more quickly than she would under normal circumstances. Therefore the remaining one third of your air supply might not be enough for both of you in such a situation.

An inexperienced diver's movements in many overhead environments can sometimes disturb sand or bottom sediments, obliterating the visibility and making it difficult for her to find her way on the return trip. Divers have learned techniques to improve safety in these conditions. These techniques include configuring equipment to reduce the likelihood that it will drag on the bottom and disturb sediments. Other techniques include using an exaggerated knee bend so the thrust of each kick is up and away from the bottom, almost like a frog kick (see figure 13.1). This kick modification is much different than the standard flutter or dolphin kicks that are taught in entry-level diving courses and used by most open-water divers.

It may be obvious, and we've said it before, but it is worth saying again: If something unexpected occurs, don't panic. *Stop. Take a deep breath and think before you act.* If you have lost your buddy in a cave, a wreck, or under ice, look and listen for your buddy and follow all established and practiced safety procedures or protocols to exit the situation safely.

After analyzing cave-diving deaths, cave-diving pioneer Sheck Exley noted three causes that showed up in nearly all of those deaths. Later, the National Speleological Society Cave Diving Section (NSS-CDS) training chairman Wes C. Skiles added two more common factors in all deaths (Exley, 1986). These were originally distributed as the Five Rules of Accident Analysis.

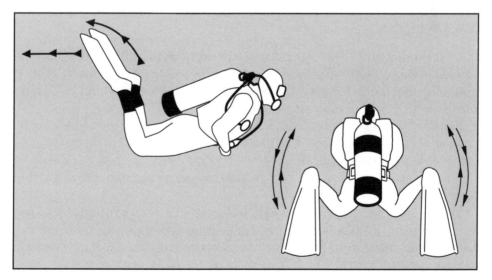

FIGURE 13.1 Use a frog kick, or similar alternative, to direct the force of your fin kicks away from the bottom to avoid stirring up silt when diving in an overhead environment.

These rules, however, apply to any dive in an overhead situation, not just cave dives. Following is the expanded version that has been developed over the years:

Expanded Rules of Accident Analysis

1. Be properly trained and equipped for the type of dive you are planning.
2. Maintain a continuous (no gaps between lines) guideline to open water.
3. Reserve two thirds of your gas supply to exit.
4. Stay within the depth range of your breathing gas to limit your risk to acceptable levels.
5. Carry two or more backup lights per diver.
6. Dive with a properly trained and equipped partner.
7. Maintain dive team continuity.
8. Increase the complexity and task loading of your dives slowly, as your experience increases.

Stated briefly, you need to acquire proper training for the dive situation, be sure that you and your buddy are prepared for the dive, and practice and train with your buddy. It is a mistake to prepare for a dive and then change your dive partner or the dive protocol at the last minute. If you do have to change your partner or protocol at the last minute, start your preparations for the dive all over again.

A detailed description of ice, cave, and wreck diving, and the special requirements for each, is beyond the scope of this book. We highly recommend taking specialized courses in both diving and rescuing divers in these environments. The following sections address only some of the general issues presented by each situation.

Ice Diving

If ice is present anywhere around the dive site, even if only a portion of the surface is covered with ice, you must consider the dive an under-ice dive. If you think that the ice around the edge of a body of water would be easy to break through from underneath, think again.

Before divers even get in the water, they should prepare the surface by moving snow away from the hole in a wagon wheel pattern to be used if they are unable to find the exit using only the safety line. This pattern, shown in figure 13.2, will provide a lighted path underwater for the divers to use to find their way back.

When making an ice dive, there should always be a standby or safety diver, who is prepared to enter the water and initiate a search should a diver lose contact with the safety line. The safety diver lets out a length of rope and swims in sweeping circles near the underside of the ice, looking for the missing diver.

The lost diver should stop and ascend directly to the underside of the ice. The lost diver may also want to use his knife to cut an indentation into the

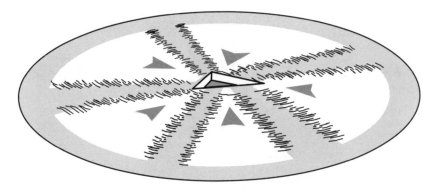

FIGURE 13.2 Scrape away the snow in a wagon wheel pattern to help a diver under the ice find his way back to the exit point.

underside of the ice to facilitate grabbing the rescue line as it goes by. The rescue diver will be on a rescue line at least one and a half times the length of the main dive line. As the rescuer swims in a circle, the rescue line will pass by the lost diver. Once the lost diver makes contact with the rescue line, he should then signal that he has been located by pulling on the line with an agreed-on sequence of rapid pulls. The surface team can then pull both the lost diver and the rescue diver to safety.

Surface team members should also be prepared to take care of rescuers as well, keeping them as comfortable as possible while they are waiting to provide assistance. Rescue divers should be seated, preferably with their feet off the ice. Wooden pallets make good insulation from the ice and provide a comfortable platform where rescue divers can sit until needed.

Cave Diving

Never enter a cave without complete training and certification for cave diving or without all of the necessary redundant equipment, including lights, regulators, and even masks. If you become separated from your dive buddy inside a cave, follow a plan for reuniting with your buddy or connecting with rescue divers. Never swim around aimlessly. Think about the situation, consider your options, and use your training. Make your moves deliberate and direct them toward resolving the situation and moving toward open water.

If the bottom has become stirred up, you should try to rise above it. Be careful, however, not to make yourself too buoyant, and don't jettison your weights. That will only pin you to the ceiling. You should turn around 360 degrees and look for your own bubbles on the ceiling or a silt trail on the bottom to determine the direction out of the cave.

Trained and experienced cavern and cave divers carry multiple light sources (see figure 13.3). While searching for your buddy, shield your light against your body and be careful not to shine the light in your buddy's face. Look around for other lights and safety lines, and listen for the sounds of other divers and searchers. You can also tap your tank and wiggle your light to attract attention.

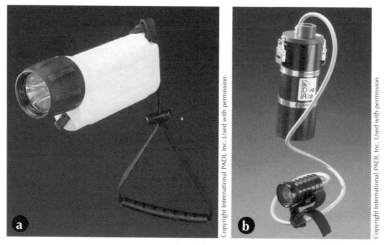

FIGURE 13.3 There are many different styles of underwater lights. When diving in an overhead environment, a diver must carry a primary light and at least one backup light.

Before you begin a methodical search for the main safety line, tie a line, possibly from your jump or gap reel, to a rock or another solid object so that you can find your way back to where you started.

If a diver becomes lost during a group cave dive, one buddy team can return to the surface to alert standby divers and get the search underway. Standby divers should bring extra air for the lost diver. The divers still in the cave should leave their safety line tied off or use a marker to show rescuers how far they made it and where to begin their search.

Never enter a cave without proper training and equipment.

Wreck Diving

Penetration of submerged wrecks is very similar to cave diving and should be approached with the same respect and caution. The same need for proper training and specialized equipment applies. One significant difference between cave diving and penetrating a wreck is that greater care must be taken inside a deteriorating wreck to avoid compounding visibility problems. Your bubbles will dislodge rust particles from the ceiling as you move, and your movements within the wreck may stir up sediment from the floor.

When diving around wrecks, take special care to maintain your visibility and orientation.

◥ Orr's Safety Stop: Specialty Training

When I first began diving in the Midwest in the early 1970s, we would travel far and wide to find and explore new dive sites. One such dive site was just outside a small town in southeastern Indiana. The rumor was that the stone quarry was filled with artifacts from the abandoned quarrying operation. Of particular interest was a mining shack that reportedly sat atop a pit and allegedly contained a treasure trove of discarded bottles and other valuable artifacts.

An exploratory dive had, indeed, located a wooden structure at a depth of about 70 feet (21 meters) in relatively clear water. Although I had years of previous diving experience, I had little or no knowledge of the techniques to be used to enter and explore a wooden building in a stone quarry. My partner and I thought it would be an easy dive for a couple of certified divers, given a little bit of thought and some modification of our diving skills. To be honest, we didn't have a clue what we were getting ourselves into.

We planned to descend to the shack and with a tether (held by my buddy on the outside). I would slip through the partially open doorway and explore the inside. After exploring the inside, I would then follow the tether to my partner on the outside. As the saying goes, it seemed like a good idea at the time.

We descended to the shack with little effort. I grabbed the end of the tether, gave my buddy the OK signal, and slid through the doorway and into the black interior of the shack. Once inside, I turned my dive light on and saw nothing but the flash of reflected silt. One of the many things we had not anticipated was that my exhaust bubbles would ascend through the roof and all the accumulated silt from the past 40 years would filter down into the shack. To make matters worse, I pulled on the tether to let my partner know that I was there only to find no resistance at the other end. As I pulled, I discovered that the end of the tether was not with my partner; both ends of the tether were inside the shack with me.

At that point, I wanted to get out of the shack and to see the open water again. Even though I was a bit anxious, I said to myself, "How difficult can this be? I'll just find a wall and move from wall to wall until I find the door." What I didn't realize was that in the zero visibility, I was actually above the top of the door; all I felt were four walls and no door.

After what seemed like an eternity, I was getting worried. By bringing my pressure gauge and light close enough to my mask,

I could see that I did not have much air left. Just then, I felt an opening, which turned out to be a circular hole about 18 inches (46 centimeters) in diameter that once held a vent pipe. The opening was large enough to put my face through so that I could see relatively clear water. For a fleeting moment, I considered removing my gear and trying to squeezing through this hole. I then realized that that idea was about as stupid as the whole experience. The clear water did have somewhat of a calming effect. I told myself to stop, take a deep breath, although I knew there weren't many deep breaths left in my tank, and think.

Having calmed down a bit, I decided to drop down a few feet and make one last attempt to find an opening. As I dropped down and made my first turn, my hand touched the top of the partially open door. Hoping it was not a door leading to another room, I slid out and into the open water. I looked around quickly for my buddy, who was nowhere in sight. There were no bubbles coming from the shack, so I decided to head for the surface, sunlight, and air.

When I surfaced, my buddy was onshore eating his lunch. After a few highly animated and colorful exchanges, my buddy admitted that the entire thing scared him. Once I went inside the shack, he wanted no part of the dive. I learned many valuable lessons that day, including the fact that diving in an overhead environment requires skills and techniques not found in open-water diver training. I also learned to be more selective when deciding on a buddy.

You should always be prepared, follow the rule of thirds regarding your air or gas supply, and run a safety line to find your way back out. When wreck diving, be aware of the presence of fishing lines, hooks, and nets hanging from the wreck, and carry two knives or cutting tools on different spots on your body in case one tool gets entangled or lost.

When entering a wreck, secure any hatches you pass through in the open position to keep surge or wave action from closing them. Be careful not to get disoriented if the wreck is sitting at an angle, making the floor look like a wall. Air pockets inside a wreck should not be considered breathable because of the presence of rust or the decomposition of cargo. As is true of any diving scenario, it is better to be aware of potential problems and prevent them than to have to deal with an accident.

Freeing Entangled Divers

Divers can become entangled in kelp, fishing line, or fishing nets. To avoid entanglements, always use extra caution when diving where fishing is popular. A lost fishing line and tackle retains its strength long after a fisherman loses it. In addition to attracting divers, wrecks and large underwater structures also attract fish. Anytime you find large populations of game fish around a dive site, you should expect to find fishing line or even fishing nets.

You can help to reduce the likelihood of entanglement by appropriately configuring and streamlining your equipment. Keep hoses, straps, and attachments in tight to your body. Monofilament fishing line in the water may be almost impossible to see, but if all of your gauges are strapped in tight, your potential to get caught up is significantly reduced. You can also turn metal clips in toward your body and tape the ends of fin straps down to make sure they don't catch anything in the water. However, be careful not to cover access to any releases or to restrict your ability to jettison weights or remove any equipment.

Some divers like to use brass snap hooks that allow them to attach equipment by simply pressing a lanyard or a metal ring against the spring closure of the hook. Unfortunately, wires, cables, and line (including fishing line) can also easily slip into these hooks, making extrication difficult if not impossible. For this reason, many divers call them "death hooks." A better design is a hook that requires the diver to open it to insert a lanyard or similar device.

If you are diving where fishing lines, nets, or kelp may be present, always carry an appropriate tool for cutting. The Z knife and others shown in figure 13.4 are particularly practical. Any cutting tool you carry should have a sharp serrated edge, a notch for cutting fishing lines, and a flat head for prying. Such

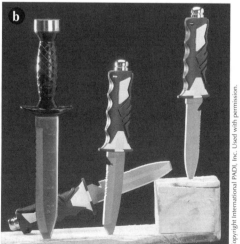

Copyright International PADI, Inc. Used with permission.

FIGURE 13.4 Use dive tools, such as *(a)* a Z knife or *(b)* other dive knives, that are practical in design and can be used for cutting, digging, and prying. Dive tools need regular maintenance so that they are ready when you need them.

a tool may not have the same psychological value as a large dive knife, but it may be infinitely more useful.

Maintain your dive knives with the same care you use for your regulator, BCD, or other life support equipment. A little cleaning and the use of appropriate lubricant after each dive will assure that, when needed, your tools will be ready and able to help. Your life and that of your buddy are certainly worth a few minutes of preventative maintenance and a cent's worth of lubricant.

◣ Orr's Safety Stop: Wire Cutters

A diver friend of mine would spend his free time exploring local farm ponds and gravel pits in and around Ohio hoping to find discarded treasure. Having heard rumors about antique telephone equipment dumped into a local lake, this friend went about trying to locate a buddy willing to jump into the less-than-appealing depths. Undeterred by the lack of a buddy and having endured strong admonishments by everyone he talked with regarding his threat to dive alone, he elected to explore the pond with ego and an overabundance of testosterone as his only dive buddies.

While feeling his way along the muddy and debris-strewn bottom, he found what he thought were wires from old telephones. They were actually abandoned coils of barbed wire. As he pulled one of the wires, one of the coils started coming uncoiled and snagged first his wetsuit, then his BCD, and then the rest of him. In a few minutes, he was hopelessly and completely ensnared in barbed wire in 15 feet (4.6 meters) of murky water, with no one there to provide any assistance. For the next hour, he spent every minute and every breath feverishly trying to extricate himself from this rusted, wetsuit-piercing, BCD-shredding death trap.

As he was taking what he was sure were his last, desperate breaths, he found that his thrashing had moved him closer to the shore. With his last bit of energy and a Herculean effort, he was able to drag himself and all that wire close enough to the surface that his lips were able to break the surface enough to get a breath. He was able to grab a tree limb in the shallow water and get enough of his upper body out of the water so that he could scream for help. A nearby farmhand ran over to help. With the aid of a pair of strong wire cutters, the farmhand was able to remove the wire. My friend was so traumatized by this near-death experience that he immediately sold his diving equipment and never returned to the sport. His experience also had a dramatic effect on his former diving partners. We made it a practice always to carry wire cutters when diving in farm ponds or local lakes where dangerous debris could have been discarded.

If you find yourself trapped by fishing line and can't get to it with a tool, you may be able to remove a piece of snagged equipment long enough to untangle it and then replace it. For example, if fishing line gets caught around your cylinder valve, you may be able to remove your BCD and untangle the line, if the diving environment permits. However, you should always try to get help from your buddy or fellow divers before removing any equipment underwater. Never remove any equipment if you aren't practiced in doing so, and even then, do it only after all other methods of dealing with the situation have failed. Although you probably learned how to doff and don your equipment underwater in your entry-level course, if you haven't practiced this skill, it may prove more challenging than you are prepared for, especially when you are under the stress of being entangled.

If you discover that your buddy or another diver is entangled, the first thing to do is calm her down. (If it happens to be you who is caught up in the entanglement, calm yourself down.) Remember—*stop, think, breathe*—and *then act*. Twisting and turning can turn a small entanglement into a serious one as the diver struggles and wraps the fishing line even more securely. Signal to the diver to be still. Reassure her with your eyes, a firm touch, and hand signals that you will take care of it. Struggling will only deplete the diver's energy and air supply and possibly lead to panic. You should also make sure the diver has an adequate air supply before you begin trying to disentangle her. If not, provide air to the diver using your alternate air source while you work on extracting her from the entanglement.

Before you start working to disentangle a diver, stop at arm's length and let the diver know your plans by using your slate or by signaling with a scissoring motion. Slowly and methodically move around the diver. Search up and down, while you check for the entanglement. Pull the diver's arms and legs free as you find the restrictions. Most of the time, you can get a diver free from the entanglement without cutting the line. While you are working to free the diver, be careful not to get tied up yourself.

If a diver is tangled up in kelp, signal to her to stop all movement. Because kelp is strongest along its axis, you can't break it by pulling on it. However, kelp is relatively weak when you bend it or snap it. It also cuts easily. Before you attempt to break or cut your buddy out of the kelp, have her try to back out the way she came in. Often, this is all it takes. Similarly, if you find yourself caught by something underwater, you should first attempt to loosen the entanglement by backing up. Swim backward, or push yourself backward with your arms and hands if the entanglement is on your legs.

14

Dangerous
Marine Life

Serious injuries caused by marine animals are extremely rare. Considering how many swimmers and divers are in the water and how many divers have uneventful and thoroughly enjoyable experiences, it is not difficult to understand that the risk and the incidence rate of injury is extremely low.

Very few marine animals are really dangerous or interested in humans at all, and fewer still are likely to get close enough to cause harm. In general, if you leave them alone, they will leave you alone. Most often, divers get injured when they have done something to provoke a defensive reaction on the part of the animal or have inadvertently put a hand or other extremity where they shouldn't. A moray eel normally bites only when you stick a hand into its hole; a stingray normally stings only when you step on it while walking into the water. Injuries caused by dangerous marine life can be broken into three categories: envenomations, irritations, and bites.

Envenomations

An envenomation takes place when a marine animal stings a diver and deposits venom. The venom is typically delivered with a spine, as in the case of a stingray, stone fish, or sea urchin. Hundreds of venomous animals in the ocean deliver venom this way. An even more common envenomation, though, can occur when a diver encounters a jellyfish. The jellyfish's tentacles deliver venom when they come in contact with the diver.

FOOD POISONING

Although it is not one of the three main categories of marine life injuries, food poisoning is an often overlooked danger of marine life. Eating undercooked or improperly prepared seafood can lead to seafood poisoning. This is a concern for divers because some of the symptoms of seafood poisoning mimic some of the symptoms of decompression illness. Symptoms to be especially concerned with are headache, abdominal cramps and burning, paralysis, muscle and joint aches, and reversal of hot and cold sensations. Other symptoms are abdominal distress—including diarrhea, vomiting, and nausea—as well as dizziness, chills, fever, and tingling around the mouth and lips.

If you believe a diver has seafood poisoning, you should monitor the diver's airway and breathing and treat for shock if the diver loses consciousness. Save the fish the diver ate, or, if the diver vomits, save the vomitus for analysis. You should get the ill person into the EMS system and consult a physician for further evaluation in case the symptoms are signs of decompression illness rather than seafood poisoning.

Spine Punctures

A diver who has received venom from a spine will have a wound that looks like a puncture or laceration (see figure 14.1). The skin will look purple or red and may be swelling. The diver may also be nauseated or vomiting. He may go into shock or into respiratory distress or arrest.

When a diver has received a venomous spine puncture, you should first remove the protruding portion of the spine and related debris with tweezers. Be careful not to dig and try to pull out the entire spine, however; spines are usually made of calcium carbonate and prone to crumbling when pulled on. You will only make the wound worse by attempting to pull the entire spine out.

To counteract the venom, immerse the wound in hot water—around 113 °F (45 °C), not so hot as to cause scalding or other heat-related injuries—for 30 to 90 minutes. During this immersion, remove the wound from the water every 10 to 15 minutes for a few minutes. If the pain and burning sensation from the venom returns, return the wound to the water.

Once you have denatured the venom, scrub the affected area with soap and water and then irrigate it vigorously with freshwater. Consult a doctor about removing the rest of the spine.

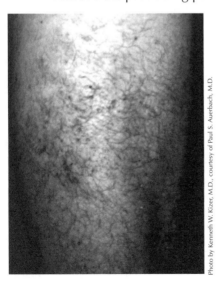

Photo by Kenneth W. Kizer, M.D., courtesy of Paul S. Auerbach, M.D.

FIGURE 14.1 A spine puncture.

Jellyfish Stings

Jellyfish deliver venom through nematocysts, tiny stinging cells on their tentacles that fire when they brush against an object. Any accidental contact will cause the cells to discharge their venom. Although most jellyfish are not big enough, nor is their venom strong enough, to immobilize or kill a diver, a diver who has an allergic reaction to the venom could be in trouble. Certain types of jellyfish, however, have sufficiently strong venom to kill humans. Jellyfish of greatest concern include the Portuguese man-o-war and box-type jellyfish such as the sea wasp or irukandji in the Indo-Pacific Ocean (see figure 14.2). When diving in this region, you should be on the lookout for these large jellyfish and their dangling tentacles, which may hang 20 feet (6 meters) or more below the body of the animal itself. When planning a dive in the Indo-Pacific Ocean, prepare yourself by researching local treatment protocols and learning whether the area you plan to dive in is known to have box jellyfish present.

A jellyfish sting usually manifests as redness or a rash, welts, swelling, or blisters; additionally, the diver may complain of a stinging or burning feeling. In the case of one of the rare jellyfish whose venom is strong enough to seriously hurt a human, the diver may become unresponsive, suffer from respiratory distress or arrest, or go into cardiac arrest. Be sure to accurately identify the type of jellyfish that inflicted the injury.

When caring for a diver who has been stung by a jellyfish, begin by flushing the injury with large amounts of seawater to remove any remaining tentacles. Jellyfish tentacles do not have to be attached to the animals to remain dangerous. Then immerse the affected area in hot water for 30 to 90 minutes to neutralize the unfired nematocysts. You can then remove the tentacles with forceps or tweezers and shave the area with shaving cream and a safety razor to remove any final hint of the tentacles or the nematocysts. Apply hydrocortisone lotion or cream to the injury to reduce the itching and irritation.

If the diver encountered a dangerous box-type jellyfish, soak the afflicted area with household vinegar or other mild acetic acid. This neutralizes any remaining stinging cells on the skin so that they are no longer a danger. Be careful when rinsing the skin with freshwater or vinegar if portions of the tentacles are still in contact with the diver's skin; any remaining intact nematocysts may sting the diver.

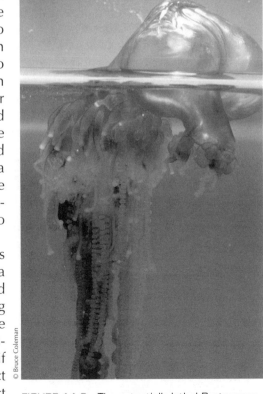

© Bruce Coleman

FIGURE 14.2 The potentially lethal Portuguese man-o-war.

Serious Envenomations

A few venomous animals, besides the aforementioned Portugese man-o-war and box-type jellyfish, are deadly. Fortunately, like many marine animals, they are not aggressive or frequently encountered. They are typically found only in the South Pacific. An encounter with the blue-ringed octopus, a venomous sea snake, or some species of cone shell may result in a life-threatening emergency. All three have strong venoms that may quickly incapacitate a person. Antivenins are available for some sea snake bites, so you should try to identify the type of snake that caused the bite. The location of antivenins should be part of your emergency assistance plan when traveling in areas where such animals are found.

A pressure immobilization bandage can delay the venom's spread in the body if the wound is on an extremity. To prepare a pressure immobilization bandage, place a dressing over the wound and then wrap an elastic bandage around the extremity, starting closest to the heart and working away from it, covering the wound for 6 inches (15.2 centimeters) on either side. Make sure that there is still adequate circulation beyond the bandage though. Be careful not to restrict circulation beyond the bandage. After the pressure bandage is in place, splint the extremity, put a sling in place to limit its movement, and then seek medical evaluation. Envenomations from animals with strong venom can be extremely serious and should be treated as emergencies.

A diver with allergic sensitivities may have an allergic reaction to venom that would not normally be classified as dangerous. The diver will display or complain of weakness; dizziness; flushed, itching, or burning skin; swelling around the face, eyes, neck, and tongue; nausea; a decreased level of responsiveness; respiratory distress or arrest; or cardiac arrest. A severe allergic reaction can actually occur with any venomous irritation or sting.

In the event of an allergic reaction, monitor the diver's airway and breathing and treat her for shock, including providing oxygen. You can also give the diver any medicine she may carry, such as Benadryl or epinephrine in the form of an EpiPen. This diver should immediately seek medical attention whether or not there are lingering symptoms.

Irritations

Irritations caused by marine animals are probably the most common marine animal injury, second only to jellyfish stings. These include cuts and abrasions caused by accidental contact with coral or anemones. Another frequent irritation is caused by brushing against hydroids that may live on permanent anchor lines on mooring buoys or other permanent structures underwater.

Divers should always wear appropriate exposure protection underwater, including gloves when appropriate. They should take care holding on to anchor lines or buoy lines when making ascents and descents, because small marine animals may live on permanent moorings and drifting jellyfish may get caught by anchor lines. In some places, local regulations do not allow divers to wear gloves. This is to discourage them from touching reefs. In this situation, divers need to be even more careful when making ascents to avoid touching objects underwater. If you wear gloves, be careful not to touch your exposed skin because stinging cells from hydroids may be on your gloves.

A cut or abrasion caused by a marine animal may be bleeding, red, swollen, or uncomfortable. Because wounds can become infected due to bacteria commonly found in ocean water, they should be monitored very closely for signs of infection such as redness, pus, swelling, a foul smell, or fever. If any of these symptoms appear, the diver should seek expert medical attention.

When dealing with irritations, cuts, or abrasions, you should control any bleeding and then irrigate the wound with sterile water or saline solution to clean it out. You can use tweezers to remove any visible debris. Afterward, cover the wound with a sterile dressing and bandage. In general, wet skin is not as effective a barrier to infection, so all abrasions should be monitored closely.

© Getty Images

To prevent irritations, avoid touching coral as well as other places where marine life may live.

Bites

Many marine animals can, and will, bite if they feel threatened. Nevertheless, the number of times humans are bitten by marine animals in a given year is extremely small. Marine animals with teeth, and many with bony mouths such as turtles, are capable of biting, given the right circumstances. But the animals that are most likely to bite include sharks, eels, barracuda and other predatory fish, seals, and sea lions.

When a bite happens, the primary concern is to control bleeding. In the water, blood loss may appear dramatic because the blood disperses in the water. Even in the water, bleeding can be controlled using direct pressure. Any debris remaining in the wound can be dislodged with saline water, a catheter, and a syringe. As with irritations, the wound should be irrigated and cleaned out and then dressed to protect it from further contamination.

© Pete Atkinson/Photographer's Choice/Getty Images

Although bites are rare, exercise caution around sharks and other predatory marine life.

◣ Orr's Safety Stop: Moray Eel

A few years ago an instructor I know was leading a group of new divers who were also very committed environmentalists. On their first ocean tour, the instructor wanted to make sure they saw as much animal life as possible. She led them to a reef where others frequently fed the fish. A nice spotted moray eel there especially liked Vienna sausages. When the instructor pointed out the eel to the new divers, she did so with bare hands. The eel, perhaps thinking the fingers were those yummy sausages, quickly clamped down on two of her outstretched fingers and held on.

The divemaster abandoned his position at the back of the group and attempted to assist the instructor, but no amount of pressure would make the eel let go. The divemaster, unable to come up with an alternative plan, whipped out his trusty, and rather rusty, dive knife and quickly dispatched the writhing eel. While several new divers learned how to wretch through their regulators, the instructor struggled to get the remainder of the eel off her fingers. Luckily, no tendons in her hand were damaged. The final result was a little scarring on the hand of the instructor and on the nerves of the divers who witnessed the experience.

Although this is a bizarre case of a marine animal injury, the first aid action was the same as in any injury. The divemaster cleaned the wound thoroughly and monitored the instructor for signs of infection. He also reassured the other divers that the incident was most likely a case of mistaken identitiy and not evil intent on the part of the eel.

Avoiding Dangerous Marine Life Injuries

As mentioned, most injuries from hazardous marine life are caused by mistakes on the part of the diver, not aggressiveness or some malevolent act on the part of the animal. Always follow standard safe diving practices and be a responsible diver. Practice buoyancy control skills and be aware of your surroundings so that you don't touch coral or anything else that could cause harm. Always look up and around when ascending so that you don't head straight into a jellyfish. Shuffle your feet and wear thick-soled boots when walking in shallow water to scare off stingrays that may be resting in the sand. Also, avoid carrying speared fish in areas where large predators such as barracuda may be present.

Educate yourself about the hazardous marine life that inhabit the area where you will be diving, and know what to avoid. A good fish identification course is highly recommended, especially when traveling somewhere new. You should also wear appropriate exposure protection, including dive skins and possibly gloves in warm water, and be passive when interacting with marine life.

15

Freediving

A text on scuba diving rescues and other aquatic emergencies wouldn't be complete without a discussion of freediving, sometimes referred to as snorkeling or skindiving. *Freediving* encompasses all methods of diving with only a mask, snorkel, and fins, but the term is frequently used for swimming in which divers spend more time underwater—exploring, hunting, or participating in competitive breathholding events. *Snorkeling* is commonly used to refer to swimming with the same equipment on the surface, exploring a shallow reef from above and occasionally swimming down to get a closer look while holding your breath.

Learning to snorkel may be a precursor to learning to scuba dive, or it may be considered a sport in its own right. Snorkeling is a popular activity with tourists in resort areas. Many scuba divers also snorkel from time to time. They have the basic equipment and generally have a love for the water. It simply stands to reason that when scuba diving isn't practical and they have an opportunity to go snorkeling, they do. Many scuba divers also use snorkeling as an opportunity to get comfortable with their equipment and adjust their buoyancy prior to a scuba dive. However, snorkeling comes with its own set of hazards brought on by inexperience or a lack of formal training in the use of the equipment.

In recent years, freediving has gained popularity and a lot of media attention. Free swimming below the water's surface is not a new activity, however. There were clubs of skindivers years before the first self-contained underwater breathing apparatus (SCUBA) was invented. Experienced freedivers have long been able to dive 60 feet (18.3 meters) or deeper and hold their breath for minutes at a time to hunt fish or to collect shellfish or lobster. In recent years, however, divers have been pushing the limits and going to depths far deeper than anyone ever considered possible.

◣ Orr's Safety Stop: Inexperience

Many years ago, I worked as the manager of a popular dive site in Ohio. Part of my responsibility was to maintain safety standards amid the hordes of visiting divers. During my tenure, I provided assistance to more than one person who had more testosterone than sense. On one such an occasion, a local youth was foundering a few feet offshore having convinced himself that he could get to the bottom of the 35-foot (10.6-meter) quarry with his rented mask, snorkel, fins, and skindiving vest but no previous snorkeling or skindiving experience.

Once I recognized that he was in distress and not just faking, I jumped in and detonated the CO_2 cartridge on his skindiving vest. I also quickly checked to see whether he was wearing a weight belt, which he was not. When I looked at him below the surface, in the limited visibility, all I saw was his white swimsuit. His vest inflated properly, but he still struggled with his arms to stay on the surface. He was in imminent danger of drowning despite a fully inflated skindiving vest.

Finally, I grabbed the back of his skindiving vest and struggled to drag him to shore. When I could stand, I continued to drag him in the extremely shallow water, perplexed about why I was having so much difficulty with someone who should be positively buoyant. I discovered, much to his embarrassment, that the white swimsuit was actually his underwear. His shorts were down around his ankles with nearly 20 pounds (9 kilograms) of lead stuffed into the pockets of his cutoff jeans!

In competitive freediving, records are classified according to equipment and means of ascending and descending. Some freedivers swim down just as the average snorkeler does, using just a mask and fins without changing their weight or using aids to descend. In other cases, freedivers ride a weighted sled to the bottom and then return to the surface riding a rapidly expanding lift bag filled with air. According to the International Association for Development of Apnea (AIDA), the current world depth record for a freediver ascending with mask and fins (or a single-blade fin with foot pockets for both feet) and constant weights is 357 feet (109 meters) for a man and 282 feet (86 meters) for a woman (AIDA International). In the no-limits category, using any means at their disposal to descend and ascend, men have reached 600 feet (183 meters) and women have reached 524 feet (160 meters). That is an astounding four times deeper than recreational scuba diving depth limits!

Regardless of the method for descending, whether you are enjoying a shallow reef, hunting game, or freediving competitively, the pressures and effects on your body are the same. You are descending through the water on a single breath of air, increasing the ambient pressure on your body, and using the oxygen contained in that breath as you work to swim.

Freediving Dangers

The pressure surrounding the body increases as a person descends through the water, doubling at 33 feet (10 meters) and tripling another 33 feet (10 meters) later. As the pressure increases, the volume of air in the lungs decreases. Freedivers have to equalize their air spaces (ears and sinuses) when they descend, just as scuba divers do. But unlike scuba divers, freedivers have limited air for equalization (i.e., the air in their lungs). This can become a problem when the freediver begins to make his ascent and returns to normal surface pressures. While at depth, the air molecules in his lungs are forced together. A freediver who stays at depth and, through normal metabolic processes, uses up the oxygen in his lungs could experience a dramatic drop in oxygen partial pressure when he ascends and the surrounding pressure drops. This drop in pressure could lead to a situation called shallow-water blackout (see figure 15.1). During the ascent, the freediver might get quite close to the surface before the oxygen partial pressure in his blood drops to hypoxic levels, causing unconsciousness. This can quickly lead to drowning if no one is close by to provide assistance and rescue the freediver, if necessary.

Experienced freedivers do their breath-hold dives singly with the aid of a buddy. One diver swims down while the buddy waits and watches on the surface. If the diver who is underwater gets into trouble, someone is available to perform a rescue. This simple system can reduce the likelihood of a freediver going missing. Unfortunately, freedivers sometimes decide to go out by themselves, and buddies sometimes fail to watch carefully, and that is when problems arise.

Several other factors may cause a freediver to need rescue. Surface conditions are sometimes unpredictable. Currents on the surface and underwater can change quickly and unpredictably. Freedivers can get themselves into trouble when they don't understand and pay attention to water and weather conditions. Just as with scuba diving, a poor or incomplete understanding of the conditions in the area can result in

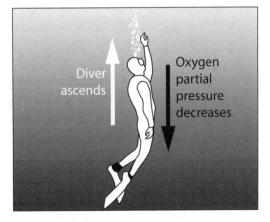

FIGURE 15.1 As a freediver ascends to the surface, the pressure on his body decreases, causing the partial pressure of the oxygen in his body to decrease rapidly. Should the freediver become unconscious close to the surface, he could sink and drown.

a diver being unable to return to his designated exit point, thereby increasing the risk of injury or death.

Dr. Duke Scott, Medical Advisor for YMCA Scuba, has created a list of Dos and Don'ts for freedivers. The following tips, from the journal *Currents*, highlight ways freedivers can avoid trouble in the first place:

Don'ts

1. Never hyperventilate vigorously prior to breath-hold diving—no more than four slow and controlled breaths.
2. Never breath-hold dive alone.
3. Never exceed your ability, go deeper, or stay down longer than your physical condition and training permit.
4. Never practice breath-hold diving in any body of water without a knowledgeable observer.
5. Never perform recreational breath-hold diving after inhaling pure oxygen, Nitrox I or II, or any other gas, except air.
6. Never breath-hold dive in cold or murky water without sufficient, prior training.

Dos

1. Always breath-hold dive with a buddy. One knowledgeable diver should be on the surface as an observer at all times.
2. Always fly a dive flag when breath-hold diving in open water.
3. Always limit pre-breath-hold dive hyperventilation to no more than four breaths and then fill the lung to approximately 80 percent lung volume.
4. Always avoid unnecessary or excessive exertion during breath-hold dives.
5. Always wear a flotation device.
6. Always review the danger of shallow-water blackout as part of your predive plan.
7. Always limit your maximum breath-hold dive time to no longer than your surface breath-hold time.

Reprinted, by permission, from D. Scott, 1999, "Shallow water blackout," *Currents* Q (3).

Freediving Between Scuba Dives

Recreational divers sometimes spend time snorkeling or freediving either between or following scuba dives. This practice is not recommended by scuba diving safety experts. In a recent workshop on breath-hold diving, a panel of medical experts supported recent recommendations against doing breath-hold

Although many divers enjoy both sports, freedives and scuba dives should not be mixed.

dives either between or immediately following scuba dives (Lindholm, Pollock, Lundgren, 2006). A growing body of evidence indicates that decompression sickness (DCS) can be induced by repeated deep breath-hold diving (Schipke, Gams, Kallweit, 2006). Breath-hold dives in conjunction with scuba dives could increase the risk of DCS, either by altering the inert gas uptake and elimination patterns or by promoting the arterialization of bubbles normally trapped in the pulmonary circuit.

Freediving Rescue Techniques

The procedures for rescuing freedivers do not differ that much from those for rescuing scuba divers. If you are the support diver for a freediver, look for the following signs that may indicate a shallow-water blackout:

- The diver stops swimming on ascent.
- The diver's legs stop moving.
- The diver's arms fall to his sides.
- The diver's eyes close or roll back in his head.
- The diver's head rolls forward or drops onto his chest.
- The diver starts sinking.
- The diver starts twitching or having spasms.

Some freedivers, typically more advanced divers or professionals, wear a wetsuit or a dive skin for thermal and exposure protection. They often wear weights to counteract the buoyancy of the wetsuit. Freediving while wearing a wetsuit can be problematic for divers who are inexperienced with the compression of neoprene at depth. Remember, the increased water pressure at depth can make a diver negatively buoyant, increasing the work required to return to the surface.

In a rescue situation, you will want to make the freediver buoyant to get her to the surface, just as with a scuba diver. By dropping her weights, you should be able to swim the diver up. Some freedivers may have small-volume buoyancy compensators as well that you can inflate orally to aid in the ascent, and some skindiving vests have a CO_2 cartridge quick-inflation mechanism for surface use in a lifesaving scenario. Triggering this cartridge releases enough CO_2 into the vest to completely inflate it and make the diver buoyant. Such vests are not commonly used today. As with any piece of diving equipment, a lack of proper maintenance and care can render a vest unreliable. A new device being worn by some freedivers is called the freediver's safety vest. It is a device programmed to inflate automatically underwater when the diver exceeds her planned depth or dive time or when she begins sinking and to bring her to the surface in a faceup position.

To rescue and ascend with a freediver, you can use either the do-si-do position or the from-behind position as described in chapter 7, Underwater Rescue Techniques. There is little chance of a lung overexpansion injury with a freediver rescue unless the diver has breathed from a scuba regulator or is carrying a pony bottle or Spare Air. Air in the freediver's lungs would return to surface volume.

Once the freediver is on the surface, get her in a horizontal, faceup position and initiate the basic care discussed in chapter 6. If you are able to get a freediver who has blacked out to the surface quickly, she may begin breathing spontaneously once returned to surface pressure. To begin your care, ensure that she has an open airway; look, listen, and feel for breathing; and begin delivering rescue breaths if necessary while towing her to the boat or to shore.

You may not be able to perform rescue breathing on a freediver who is not breathing. If the diver's airway has been exposed to water, a condition known as laryngospasm may occur, in which the larynx goes into spasm to keep the diver from inhaling water. Keep attempting rescue breathing because eventually the laryngospasm will relax and you will be able to get breaths in. The diver may also begin breathing on her own.

If the freediver is conscious on the surface and struggling or panicking, you will need to be just as cautious as with a panicking scuba diver. A freediver might not have the appropriate equipment to maintain or establish buoyancy on the surface. She may not have weights you can drop.

As with any panicked diver on the surface, an in-water rescue should be your last choice. Before going out yourself, use the "reach, throw, or row" steps discussed in chapter 6. Whatever you decide to do, don't endanger your own life attempting to make a rescue. That would only put two people at risk and make it more difficult for other rescuers. If you aren't able, trained, or equipped to make an in-water rescue, contact the authorities and wait for someone who is.

Caring for an Unconscious Freediver

Regardless of what brought you to the emergency situation, whether it was a shallow-water blackout or panic on the surface, if the freediver is unconscious when you are providing care, the rules of basic life support apply. If you were providing rescue breaths while you towed the diver toward help, once you are on shore or on a boat you will need to open the airway; look, listen, and feel for breathing; and assess signs of circulation. Always take a moment to reassess the diver's situation after you have him out of the water.

Treat an unconscious freediver as a possible drowning. Your first priority will be to begin breathing for the diver. There is no point in trying to drain or empty water from the freediver's mouth or airway. He may or may not have inhaled any water. If he did, there is nothing you can do about it as a first responder. What he does need, though, is oxygen.

Begin delivering rescue breaths. If the freediver does not exhibit signs of circulation, and you are on shore, on a boat, or on another hard surface, combine the rescue breaths with chest compressions to provide full cardiopulmonary resuscitation. That will deliver the much-needed oxygen to the freediver and get it circulating throughout his body.

You can increase the concentration of inspired oxygen, once you are back on shore or onboard a boat, by connecting your emergency oxygen unit to the pocket-style mask and delivering rescue breaths with supplemental oxygen. Doing so puts the amount of oxygen delivered to the diver in the range of 50 percent, as opposed to 16 percent provided by rescue breaths alone. The details of performing CPR and providing emergency oxygen first aid are discussed in chapter 11, Diving First Aid.

If the freediver begins breathing on his own, switch him to a nonrebreather mask and continue providing oxygen at up to 15 liters per minute. In this situation, though, you should closely monitor the freediver to ensure that he doesn't relapse and stop breathing. Typically, because snorkelers and freedivers who have nearly drowned will not be able to activate a demand valve, you won't be able to use that device to provide emergency oxygen.

You should immediately get the freediver into the EMS system. Even if a diver who recovers in the water tells you that he feels better, he should be assessed by professional medical care providers to prevent secondary drowning, a condition in which the water that enters a freediver's lungs has caused damage that impairs the lungs' ability to process oxygen.

EPILOGUE

Diving accidents are, as we have indicated in this book, a relatively rare occurrence, and most divers will enjoy their entire diving career without ever being involved in a rescue. Although the odds are that you will never be called upon to participate in the rescue of another diver, you should be prepared nonetheless. Scuba lifesaving techniques should be taught and practiced at all levels of scuba certification and training and should be reinforced at every opportunity so that the skills are maintained at the most proficient level. After all, you never know when circumstances may arise in which you are called upon to come to the aid of a buddy or a fellow diver in distress.

Knowledge and the proper application of recently practiced skills are probably the most important diving safety tools you can use to manage the risks associated with diving. The more you know and the more frequently you practice your diving and rescue skills, the better prepared you will be to manage virtually anything that may happen during a dive.

Eric and I hope that your next dive, and every dive thereafter, will be the most exciting and rewarding experience you have ever had.

You overcome adversity not by physical strength
but by the effective application of knowledge and skill.

—*Dan Orr*

REFERENCES

AIDA International. World Records. www.aida-international.org.

American Heart Association. 2005. *Guidelines for cardiopulmonary resuscitation and emergency cardiovascular care.* Dallas, TX: American Heart Association.

American Psychiatric Association. 1994. *Diagnostic and statistical manual of mental disorders.* 4th ed. Washington, DC: American Psychiatric Association, 394-403.

Caruso, J.L. 2004. Caution first: Why cigarette smoking and diving don't mix. *Alert Diver* (July/August): 42-43.

Caruso J.L., D.M. Uguccioni, J.E. Ellis, J.A. Dovenbarger, and P.B. Bennett. 2004. Do divers in trouble drop their weight belts or integrated weights? A look at the ditching of weight. *Undersea and Hyperbaric Medicine* 31: 307.

Colvard, D.F., and L.Y. Colvard. 2003. A study of panic in recreational scuba divers. *The Undersea Journal,* first quarter, 40-44.

Divers Alert Network. 2005. *Report on decompression illness, diving fatalities and Project Dive Exploration.* Durham, NC: Divers Alert Network.

Divers Alert Network. 2006. *Report on decompression illness, diving fatalities and Project Dive Exploration.* Durham, NC: Divers Alert Network.

Exley, S. 1986. *Basic cave diving: A blueprint for survival.* Lake City, FL: National Speleological Society.

Ladd, G., V. Stepan, and L. Stevens. 2002. The Abacus Project: Establishing the risk of recreational scuba death and decompression illness. *South Pacific Underwater Medicine Society Journal* 32:124-128.

Lindholm, P., N.W. Pollock, and C.E.G. Lundgren, eds. 2006, June 20-21. Breath-hold diving. *Proceedings of the Undersea and Hyperbaric Medical Society/Divers Alert Network Workshop.* Durham, NC: Divers Alert Network.

Pollock, N.W., D.M. Uguccioni, and G. de Lisle Dear, eds. 2005, June 19. Diabetes and recreational diving: Guidelines for the future. *Proceedings of the Undersea and Hyperbaric Medical Society/Divers Alert Network Workshop.* Durham, NC: Divers Alert Network.

Rodgers, T. Down to the sea: Despite death, sunken ship still open to divers. *San Diego Union-Tribune.* August 1, 2006. Retrieved January 12, 2007 from: www.signonsandiego.com/uniontrib/20060801/news_1m1yukon.html.

Rodgers, T. Overconfidence killed veteran scuba diver Steven Donathan. *San Diego Union-Tribune.* August 22, 2005. Retrieved January 12, 2007 from: www.cdnn.info/news/safety/s050822b.html.

Schipke, J.D., E. Gams, and O. Kallweit. 2006. Decompression sickness following breath-hold diving. *Res Sport Med* 14(3): 163-168.

Scott, D. Shallow water blackout. *Currents.* Retrieved January 12, 2007 from: www.ymcascuba.org/ymcascub/currnt29.html.

Sheffield, P., and R.D. Vann. 2002, May 2. Flying after recreational diving. *Proceedings of Divers Alert Network Workshop.* Durham, NC: Divers Alert Network.

Sporting Goods Manufacturers Association. 2006. *SGMA sports participation topline report.* Washington, DC: Sporting Goods Manufacturers Association.

INDEX

Note: The italicized *f* and *t* following certain page numbers refer to figures or tables, respectively.

ABOUT THE AUTHORS

Dan Orr is president and CEO of the Divers Alert Network (DAN), an international scuba diving safety organization. A veteran diver of more than 40 years, Orr joined DAN in 1991 and immediately established the DAN training department and the Oxygen for Scuba Diving course, a standard in the dive industry.

Orr has held membership and leadership positions in many notable diving organizations such as National Association of Underwater Instructors (NAUI), Professional Association of Diving Instructors (PADI), Association of Canadian Underwater Councils (ACUC), Young Men's Christian Association (YMCA), National Academy of Scuba Educators (NASE), International Association of Nitrox and Technical Divers (IANTD), Undersea & Hyperbaric Medical Society (UHMS), National Association For Cave Diving (NACD), the Historical Diving Society, Academy of Underwater Arts and Sciences, the Institute of Diving, and the Explorers Club. He is chairman of the board of the Historical Diving Society and secretary of the DEMA board of directors. He has several specialty certifications, including full cave diver, rescue diver and rapid response rescue and recovery. Orr has authored, coauthored, or reviewed more than 15 books and manuals on scuba and various aspects of scuba safety and rescue.

Eric Douglas is director of training at the Divers Alert Network (DAN), where he researches and develops dive safety training programs. He is also a diver medical technologist, a dive instructor, and master trainer for first aid and basic life support. Douglas worked for the world's largest dive training organization, the Professional Association of Diving Instructors (PADI), where he helped develop training materials and served as the assistant editor of *Undersea Journal*, a publication read by more than 150,000 professional divers worldwide. Trained as a journalist with a degree from Marshall University, Douglas has written thousands of stories and three fictional books involving diving.

More great aquatic resources available from Human Kinetics!

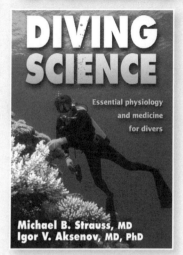
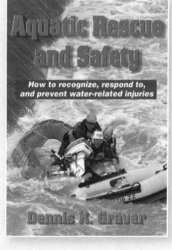
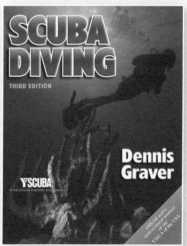